Weaving
Tricks

Weaving Tricks

Susan Gilmurray

 VAN NOSTRAND REINHOLD COMPANY
NEW YORK CINCINNATI TORONTO LONDON MELBOURNE

Printed in the United States of America

Published by Van Nostrand Reinhold Company
A division of Litton Educational Publishing, Inc.
135 West 50th Street, New York, NY 10020

Van Nostrand Reinhold Limited
1410 Birchmount Road
Scarborough, Ontario M1P 2E7, Canada

Van Nostrand Reinhold Australia Pty. Ltd.
17 Queen Street
Mitcham, Victoria 3132, Australia

Van Nostrand Reinhold Company Limited
Molly Millars Lane
Wokingham, Berkshire, England

16 15 14 13 12 11 10 9 8 7 6 5 4 3 2 1

Library of Congress Cataloging in Publication Data
Gilmurray, Susan.
    Weaving tricks.

    Bibliography: p.
    Includes index.
    1. Hand weaving. I. Title.
TT848.G56   746.1'4   80-15132
ISBN 0-442-26132-2

Acknowledgments

Over the past ten years, I have marveled at the amount of weaving information exchanged in an informal manner whenever weavers gather. With drafts, diagrams and demonstrations, kindred souls share their weaving secrets willingly.

This book is the result of personal observations and of generous contributions from weavers and weaving teachers. Those whose ideas I can identify and who were willing to share include Mary Anderson, Laya Brostoff, Estelle Carlson, Barbara DePeaux, Virginia Harvey, Kenneth Heinz, Ramona Laurence, Rosemary Malbin, Betty Nelson, Helen Pope, Ruth Rummler, Naomi Towner, and, for her many contributions, inspiration and support, Harriet Jenny.

Finally I wish to thank my husband, Frank, who has unfailingly been my closest friend. Without his support, advice and hard work, this book would have remained just a wish.

Table of Contents

Chapter 1:

Studio and Equipment

Studio Space

Soon after the weaving-bug bites, a strong desire for a home studio usually develops. A home studio doesn't have to be the monumental space of a weaver's dreams to function well. Look around your abode for a space that provides reasonable working conditions. Check for good lighting possibilities, good storage space, a bare wall for hanging work and space for your loom. A sewing room, den, family room, guest room, sun porch, heated attic or finished basement are good locations for a home studio. In older homes a large pantry set apart from the kitchen can provide excellent working space, especially if the weaver is also a dyer.

Apartments present more problems because there are so few unused spaces. A loom in the living area of an apartment dictates the decor. Any attempt to mix weaving with dust catchers like velvets, carved wood, textured carpets or exposed high fidelity equipment is bound to be frustrating and plenty dusty.

Protect record players and tape decks with appropriate dust covers. Amplifiers and televisions do best on a shelf with another shelf a few inches above the equipment to allow for adequate cooling but prevent settling dust. While you're covering things, find a cloth to cover the dressed loom to protect the work in process.

Most important, if you want to weave a lot, acknowledge the fact that you'll be spending hours in the loom room. Avoid areas that are cold, damp, too sunny or drafty. Protect yourself from allergic reactions to fiber dust by providing adequate ventilation.

After you've selected a studio space, a certain amount of work on the area will increase your weaving pleasure and improve your weaving product.

Studio Lighting

It's wise to paint your studio white or light gray if the room is sunny. Colorful walls can cause misjudgment of yarn colors by reflecting the wall color onto the yarn in question.

Studio lighting can also add unwanted tints. Natural lighting from a northern exposure is obviously ideal, but a combination of florescent fixtures and incandescent lamps also provides suitably balanced light. If only florescent fixtures are available, daylight corrected tubes should be used.

The color a room imparts to your weaving can be analyzed. Choose a piece of weaving that has a variety of colors including reds and oranges, and blues and greens. Take the weaving out into the morning sunlight and examine the brightness of the various colors. Then take the same weaving into your studio. If the blues and greens appear brighter or there is a purple cast noticeable in the reds, the room has too much ordinary florescent light. Incandescent lamps, with their characteristic yellow glow, will balance the bluish cast of a room lit entirely with ordinary florescent tubes. If the oranges and reds seem brighter and neutral colors appear golden, there is too much incandescent light or the sun's rays enter the window(s) at too low an angle in the morning for eastern exposures and in the evening for western exposures. Other than window shades, the solution to a problem window is to plan color selection for another area or for another time of day. The warm hues of early evening sun are just fine for weaving preselected colors.

Working Wall

At least one wall of the studio should be available for hanging work. A favorite solution for a working wall is to apply white, plain finish, suspended ceiling panels to the walls. Usually available in 2' × 4' pieces, these panels can be stuck to the walls with double-stick picture hangers, glued with mastic adhesive or nailed to the studs with common or roofing nails. These panels provide a marvelous surface for everything from push-pins to pencil drawing; they can be repainted with latex indoor wall paint when a clean surface is needed. A piece of picture rail molding, installed across the wall about ½" from the ceiling, will provide a ledge for "S" hook and wire hangers. Moveable track lights make the wall a mini-gallery. Peg board also provides hanging and storage possibilities.

Storage

Storage becomes a growing problem for a weaver with a craving for more and more yarn. The most obvious need is for some sort of shelving arrangement. However, shelves are not a total solution to the problems caused by dust, heat, bright light and excessive fluctuations in humidity.

Large quantities of a single material such as fleece or bulky skeins can be stored in plastic garbage bags. These bags should have a few small holes poked in them to prevent condensation in cooler weather and mildew in the summer. Cones and spools of yarn fit in clear freezer bags, shirt bags, plastic bread wrappers and vegetable bags. Wicker hampers protect yarn from dust and sun and are excellent for areas with changeable climate, since they breathe. Five-gallon cardboard drums with lids, available from ice cream shops, make perfect homes for large and unwieldy balls of yarn. Punching a hole in the center of the carton lid and feeding the end of the ball of yarn out through the hole creates a combination yarn feeder and dust proof storage container. Keep one container for thrums and small quantities of unused yarn, but keep these labeled for content and source. As time goes by, this container will evolve into a resource bin for color and texture. It can be dumped out to get ideas for a new piece or to find just the right touch for a waning design in progress.

1. Studio storage

Hat stands and expanding mug racks are good studio additions for hanging skeins and prepared warps. Coffee cans hold heddles, reed hooks, scissors and other slender pieces of equipment. The closing of a hardware store, post office or novelty shop signals the sale of bins and compartmented sorters adaptable for studio storage. Used office furniture companies offer similar storage pieces at reasonable prices.

Ask your favorite yard goods store for large, hollow tubes that some fabrics are stored on. These tubes can be converted to storage containers for lease sticks, raddles and weaving swords, or they can serve their original purpose of storing your own handmade material. A most useful addition to your storage repertoire is a roll of commercial dry cleaner's bags. A large roll of garment-sized bags lasts years and years. Look up dry cleaner's supplies in the Yellow Pages of your telephone directory.

Looms

The weaver's most necessary tool is a loom. No other piece of equipment so influences the weaver's possibilities. Thus the selection, understanding and care of a loom are essential to weaving. Appendix II contains illustrations of common looms and lists various loom parts.

Loom Buying

Buying a loom is something like buying a car—there are Cadillacs and there are compacts. It is important to know about the product in general, as well as your specific needs and the variety of options available.

The size of the loom is an easy decision based on the space available and the desired weaving width. For yard goods a good weaving width is the distance the arms can comfortably span to catch the shuttle (see Planning Yardage). Special needs such as large rugs or wall hangings make looms larger than this arm measure necessary. For very tight spaces a folding loom might be considered.

Loom Frame

Perhaps the most expensive ingredient in a good loom is the frame. Unless the loom design incorporates hefty-size wooden parts, a fine-grained, hardwood frame is desirable. The frame should be assembled with mortise and tenon, dovetail or lapped joints and secured with bolts or pegs rather than screws (Figure 2).

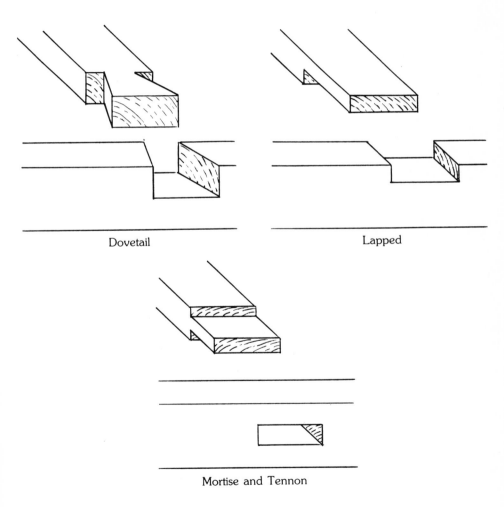

Dovetail   Lapped

Mortise and Tennon

2. Wood joints

Of the variety of looms available, the most common ones seem to be based either on an X, a V or the standard rectangular frame of many traditional looms. The V-frame is employed to advantage by folding looms where the breast and back of the loom can be closed up against the castle. Generally the X-frame is somewhat weak and suitable only for folding, lightweight looms or table loom conversions.

While you're admiring the frame, take a look at the beams (Figure 3). The cloth beam should be a good distance from other loom parts allowing thick weavings to pass around the beam. At the same time it should be positioned to allow plenty of room for treadling. Some looms have an extra knee beam that creates more space for the knees and protects the cloth from accidental damage by diverting the web.

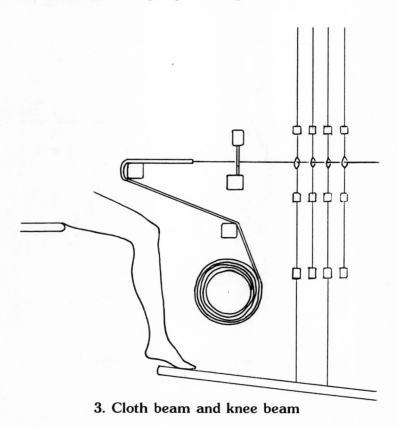

3. Cloth beam and knee beam

Both the warp and cloth beams should each have one or more tension devices (Figure 4) that combine a strong brake with ease of tensioning and backlash control. The most common systems are rachet, double rachet and friction brake. The single rachet is the least acceptable device and should be considered only in combination with a double rachet or friction brake. The double rachet is vey strong with somewhat flexible tensioning, but, like the single rachet, it is hard to control when releasing very taut warps. A warp beam will literally throw warp when a single or double rachet under extreme tension is released without auxiliary control. The friction brake allows for very fine adjustments and never lets the beam backlash; however, it won't hold an extreme tension. Therefore, many looms combine a friction brake on the warp beam with a double rachet on the cloth beam. This is generally a satisfactory combination. However, for weaving large rugs and tapestries, rachets are necessary on both beams.

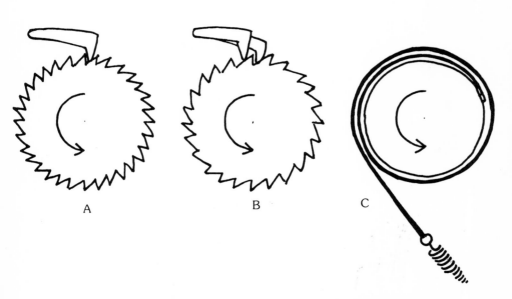

A   B   C

4. (A) Rachet, (B) double rachet and (C) friction brake

Look under the loom for a sure and easy tie-up system. Precut, pretied or preformed tie-up connectors save tie-up time. Check to see that the ties can't become tangled or wear out from rubbing loom parts. Ask for a test drive. Try weaving at least an inch. During the weaving the treadles should move freely. Inspect ties and treadles for signs of abrasion such as polished wood and metal or discolored ropes.

Some bent-wire connectors can jump out of the treadle groove while weaving is in progress if the groove and wire are not carefully manufactured. With pin and loop tie-ups a frequent tie-up problem is caused by an unsecured pin backing out of the loops. The most time-consuming system is the all-rope tie-up, which has a dubious advantage of adjustability and the real benefit of silence and traditional beauty.

Check out the harnesses and beater for smooth and convenient operation. Harness frames should be easy to lift out or otherwise remove from the loom. Any clips holding the metal strips on which the heddles ride should be easy to open and close; in short, there should be features that make it easy to add, subtract and position heddles. A well-designed beater swings easily and strikes the web at close to a right angle. A beater that beats down (or up, on the overhead beater loom) on the cloth because it pivots near the harnesses cannot produce a firm cloth. A shuttle race prevents the possibility of a shuttle nose-dive through widely spaced or unevenly tensioned warps. The beater should allow for quick installation of reeds.

The three types of heddles (Figure 5) each have their advantages. The wire heddle is the easiest to thread and move on the harness frame. The flat metal heddle allows for more ends per inch on a harness but is harder to thread than the wire heddle. The string heddle is slower to thread but has the advantage of being extremely gentle with the warps, thus allowing more variety in warps and setts.

A removable or folding breast beam facilitates the threading and sleying process (see Threading the Heddles and Sleying the Reed).

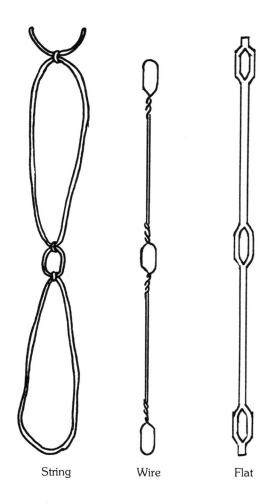

| String | Wire | Flat |

5. Three kinds of heddles

Types of Looms

The actual weaving apparatus and its "action" is the most important part of the loom. There are basically four types available. *Tapestry looms* usually have simple two shed systems controlled by string heddle or one string heddle and a flat stick in the second shed.

17

The *counterbalance loom* is the simplest mechanical form of the multiple harness loom. By balancing the harnesses against each other on rollers, an excellent shed is obtained because the harnesses move both up and down (Figure 6). The tie-up is simple: the sinking harnesses are tied to the treadles which pull them down either directly or from lams. These looms have two disadvantages involving the nature of pulleys. They have a tendency to get out of kilter if the harness ropes slip around the rollers and they are often unable to balance three rising harnesses against one sinking harness. This practically eliminates certain weaves such as tubular double weave.

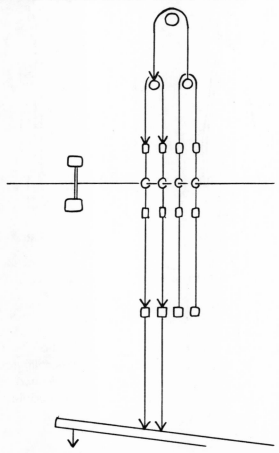

6. Counterbalance loom action

The *jack loom* moves each harness independently by either pulling or pushing up the desired harness(es). The jack loom is easy to tie-up with treadles working only the rising harnesses. The action is very stable but the treadling can be stiff and the shed shallow if the mechanical advantage is not with the weaver (Figure 7). Another possible problem with the shed is caused by the raised threads being under more tension than the threads in the bottom of the shed. This situation occurs when the manufacturer fails to account for the fact that the closed shed should actually be in a slightly sinking position. A raised back beam or a lowered harness position cures this characteristic jack loom problem.

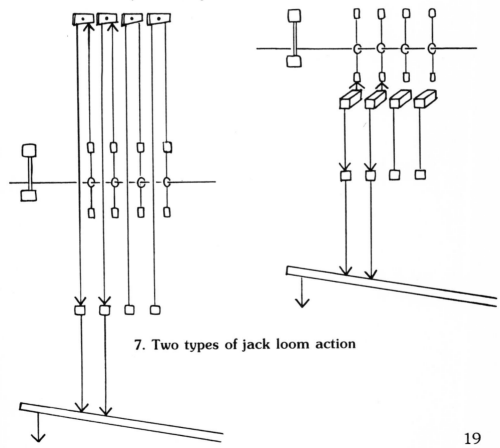

7. Two types of jack loom action

The *counter march* loom combines rising and sinking sheds and tie-up is complex because every harness has to be tied to every treadle via up and down lams. The tie-up price is small considering the advantages of independent action, good shed and easy treadling (Figure 8).

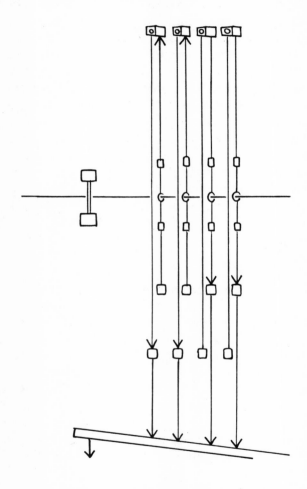

8. Counter march loom action

Mechanical Advantages

Besides a good frame and a reasonable tie-up system, a loom should require a minimum of effort to weave. The ability to move large loom parts with the touch of a toe requires mechanical advantage. Loom design can give the mechanical advantage to the weaver. Assessing the mechanics of a particular loom involves recalling and understanding a few basic physical laws.

The lever and the pulley are the real working parts of the loom. Their use and placement can make the difference between a difficult trial and a creative adventure. On looms levers are used mainly as treadles and harness lifters. Each lever has a fulcrum or fixed point. To use the lever, the object to be moved is attached as close as possible to the fulcrum while the force is applied as far as possible from the fulcrum. Thus, treadles attached at the back of the loom (the fulcrum) make the weaving easier by placing the harness to be lifted closer to the fulcrum than the foot doing the work. The reverse is true of treadles attached at the front of the loom. With the fulcrum at the front of the loom and the harness at the furthest position, more work is required to raise the harness.

Levers are also used on jack and counter march looms as harness lifters. Again, the mechanical advantage should be in the weaver's favor. The pulley-wheels or pulley-dowels of a counterbalance loom convert the natural, downward treadle movement into the upward movement of a harness.

Friction can be a mechanical disadvantage, especially when jack looms use wood-on-wood lifters to push up the harness. Friction can increase on other looms when many harnesses are worked by a complex system of lams and jacks. Each bearing surface adds to the resistance encountered in treadling.

Finally, gravity and the pendulum effect can contribute to the way the beater moves. For example, the overhead beater can be a disadvantage if it has to be pushed too far back toward the harnesses before the shuttle can be put through, or it may use gravity to advantage by gaining momentum from the swing of the beater.

Options

Many available options enhance the weaving process. Some of these options are actually features on certain makes of looms. Add-a-harness has long been associated with Macomber looms, while other manufacturers offer similar additions as options. Threading can actually be changed on the Pioneer loom while the loom remains warped. Options to consider include rubber feet to prevent "walking" on wooden floors, cloth protectors to prevent snags as the cloth passes close to the weaver around the breast beam of the loom, and pins or jigs to stabilize the harnesses while threading—especially useful on a counterbalance or counter march loom (Figure 9).

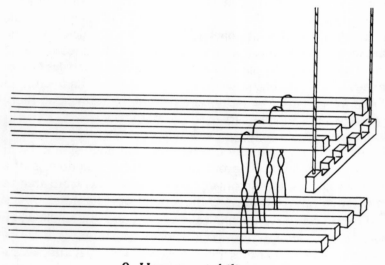

9. Harness stabilizers

The Right Loom

With all this information, the choice of a loom is far from cut and dried. There are few, if any, looms that are right for everything and, on the other hand, there are very few all-wrong looms. The secret is to match the right loom to the right job.

For example, points to look for in a loom used for weaving durable, large rugs of simple design would include a strong frame with pegged mortise and tenon joints, rachets on both beams, a counterbalance action for ease of treadling and a heavy, overhead beater to assist in pounding in the weft. The same loom might well be able to produce yardage, but a lighter, more responsive jack loom would add pleasure, speed and design advantage to yardage projects. A folding frame loom with lapped and screwed joints would also suffice for yardage; an easy brake release, fast tie-ups, knee beam and cloth protector would be good options for such a loom.

Loom Tying

No matter what kind of loom is selected, a certain amount of knot tying will be necessary to make the loom function. The most extreme example of necessary loom tying is the string heddle counterbalance or counter march loom with harnesses, lams and treadles all connected with cords that must be tied. Even the most mechanized jack loom will require knots to tie the warp to the apron.

Loom Knots

The right knot is all important to loom tying, since faulty knots are clumsy at best.

The most basic knot, the *overhand,* is the one that everybody ties to make a "bump" in one or more strings. Weavers use it to join two strings rather permanently, since the knot tightens under tension and becomes very difficult to untie. The "bump" aspect is frequently used to keep a cord from pulling through a drilled hole in a harness, lam or treadle. Because it is easy to tie and durable, it is frequently used as a fast and sturdy finished edge for weaving. To tie an overhand knot, form a loop in the string(s) and pass the end(s) through the loop and pull (Figure 10).

10. Overhand knot

The *square knot* is harder to master but is useful in loom tying because of its quick-release characteristic; it is also beautiful when worked as a macramé finish for weavings. It is made up of two of those simple knots that come before the bow in shoe laces. These half-knots are tied right over left and left over right to form one square knot (Figure 11). Two right over left half-knots form a granny knot which will not untie easily. The square knot can be used instead of a bow knot for tying warp to the apron rod, especially when the warp length is limited. By pulling on one end of the knot a double half-hitch will form around the taut end. The double half-hitch can usually be slipped off the pulled end.

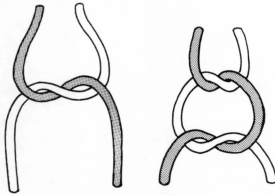

11. Square knot

The most common weaver's knot, *the snitch,* is used to connect jacks and harnesses to treadles and lams as well as lams to treadles. For each snitch knot, cut two lengths of cord, each one and a half times longer than the total distance to be spanned. Each length is folded in half; an overhand knot forms one length into a loop while the other is overhand knotted at the folded middle to leave two loose ends. Th overhand knots hold the cords in the loom parts. The looped cord is then formed into a lark's head by folding the unknotted end of the loop back on itself to make two small loops. These two small loops are folded toward each other and the loose ends of the other half of the knot pass through the lark's head. The ends are adjusted to the desired length and secured with a half knot or square knot (Figure 12).

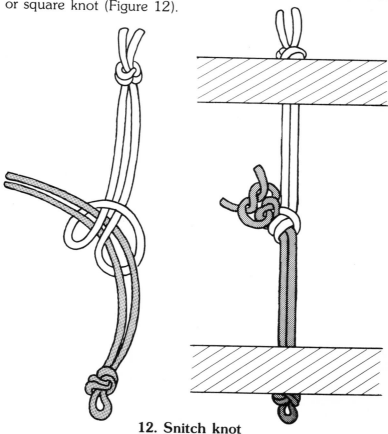

12. Snitch knot

25

The actual *weaver's knot* is called a bowline by sailors and climbers. Revered by all three callings because of its non-slip and quick release characteristics, it can be used anywhere two cords are tied together or to fasten one cord to a loom part. The bowline is described by a climber's story. There once was a rabbit warren with a tree growing behind it and each day the rabbit would run out of his nest, around the tree and back into the hole. The rabbit warren with the tree behind it is a length of cord formed into a loop, with the cord behind the loop as the tree. The other end follows the rabbit's path. This cord comes up through the loop, goes around the cord tree and back into the loop (Figure 13).

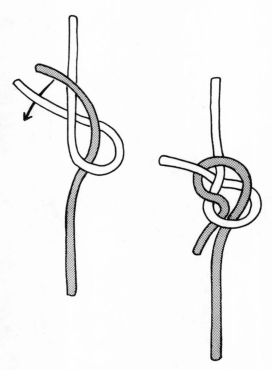

13. Weaver's knot

The *plied cord adjustable knot* is unbelievably stable but requires a plied rather than a braided cord. It is especially good for hanging harnesses because of its adjustability. The knot-forming cord is cut into a length at least one foot longer than the distance to be spanned, and one end is fixed to the upper loom part. The cord then passes through a lower attachment loop or screw eye and is pushed through an untwisted slit in the cord several inches above the lower attachment. The end is then pushed through the cord 2″ above the first intersection. The cord is adjusted and held securely with a half hitch assisted by the weight on the twisted cord (Figure 14).

Another adjustable knot, that is less knot than *friction fastener,* involves a length of cord two and one half times the desired distance to be spanned and screw eyes installed on the loom parts to be connected. A nonslip loop is first tied in one end of the cord using a weaver's knot. The unknotted end is then passed through the first and second screw eyes, through the cord loop and tied in a weaver's knot to the second screw eye (Figure 15).

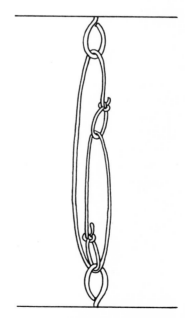

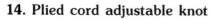

14. Plied cord adjustable knot   **15. Adjustable friction fastener**

Counterbalance Harness Balance

Four-harness counterbalance harness balance, the nemesis of novice weavers, can be cinched by using only the best loom tying cord or sash cord and by literally starting at the top. Enlisting the help of a friend speeds up the job and does away with the need for ropes and boards to hold the harnesses in place while you work.

To begin, position one harness so that the heddle eyes are in a line with the tops of the back and breast beams. Next measure the distance from the castle roller to the top of the aligned harness. Divide this measurement in half and use the resulting figure to position the secondary rollers or heddle horses which should be halfway between the castle rollers and the harnesses. To hang the heddle horses, attach loom tying cords of twice the hanging distance plus 18″ approximately 4″ from each end of one heddle horse. Pass the cords over and around the roller and fasten both cords to the second heddle horse. When the heddle horses are tied-up parallel to the roller, secure the roller to the castle and the heddle horses to each other using string, masking tape and/or your friend.

Using the same techniques, hang all four harnesses and, after they are adjusted in line with the breast and back beam and parallel to the rollers, secure them to each other (Figure 16). This is a good chance to use jigs, which are notched pieces of wood made especially for holding the harness frames.

Lams should be tied-up parallel to the harnesses and, finally, the treadles should be tied to the lams in a raised position determined by the depth of the shed desired and the distance between the knee and the cloth on the loom. With the loom completely tied, the securing jigs, ties and tape can be removed.

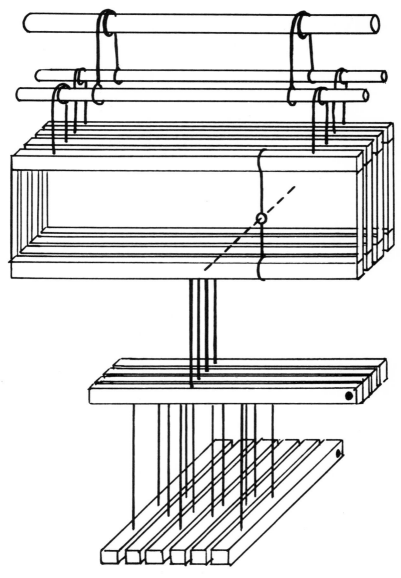

16. Hanging counterbalance harnesses

Counter March Ties

The counter march loom is tied in a fashion similar to the counterbalance loom. Beginning again at the top of the loom, secure the jacks in the level position. Using the harness jigs as rests, position the harnesses so that the eyes of the heddles are in line with the tops of the back and breast beams. Attach the upper heddle bar of each harness to the outer ends of the corresponding jacks using any adjustable knot. The bottom of each harness is attached with a snitch knot to the corresponding upper lam, which should be parallel or at a slight up-angle (Figure 17).

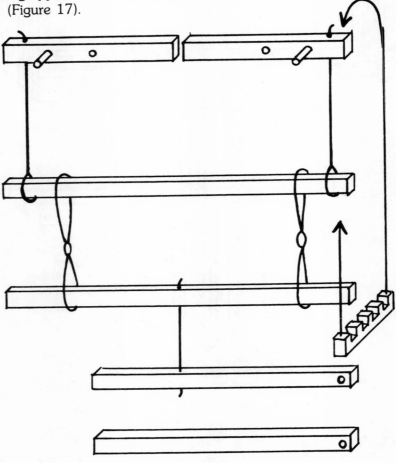

17. Attach harnesses to jacks and lams

Each pair of jacks is tied together with a drooping length of cord and then attached to the respective lower lam using a snitch to connect the droopy cord to the lam cord (Figure 18).

The treadles are tied to every harness via either the lower up-lams or the upper down-lams (Figure 19).

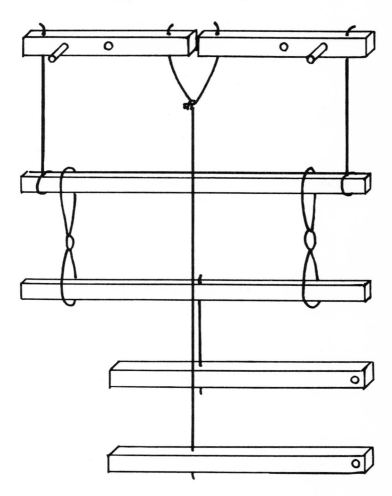

18. Attach lower lams to jacks

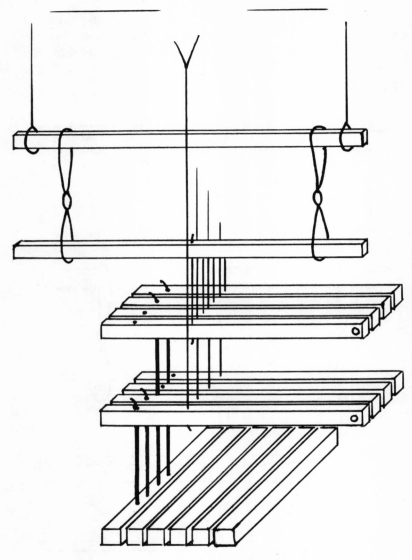

19. Counter march treadle tie-up

On long warps with a consistent pattern, the tie-up time is well worth the resulting weaving action. The fact that most four-harness weaves usually require a standard, six-treadle tie-up, makes the weaver's time spent under the loom minimal.

However there are serious tie-up problems when the weaver attempts a variety of double weaves or tubular constructions on a four-harness counter march loom. For example, without resorting to pickup sticks, a fiber construction using tabby and variations of two layers requires a total of ten treadles (Figure 20). Therefore the weaver is constantly tying and retying the recalcitrant counter march. This tie-up problem multiplies when the weaver begins to investigate multiharness weaves. Deriving an interesting tie-up for an eight harness summer and winter can take hours under the loom. Producing a multilayer construction is nearly impossible.

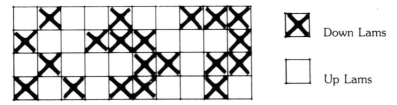

Down Lams

Up Lams

20. Counter march tubes tie-up

For these reasons a new way to tie-up for experimental work to explore treadling possibilities is necessary. A simple jack tie-up using only the lower lams proves to be most unsatisfactory. The delightful rising and sinking action is lost and the resulting shed is shallow with the nonsinking lower shed barely able to support a shuttle.

However, a working jack tie-up solution is possible with a very minor modification in the lams. For every pair of upper and lower lams, a large rubber band is utilized (Figure 21). For small looms, a ¼"-wide rubber band will do. For larger looms, ½" waistband elastic works well. For very large looms with tight, wide warps, 1" strips of tire inner tube are perfect.

33

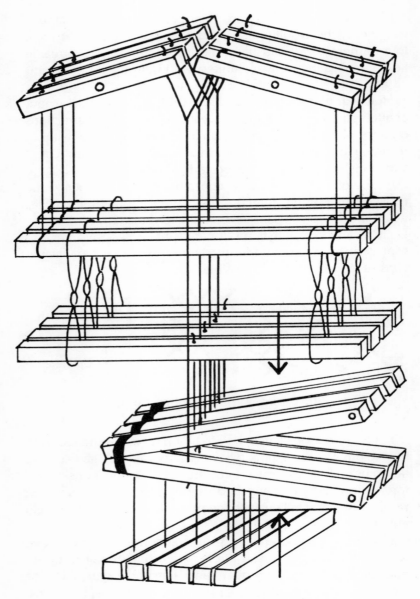

21. Rubber band counter march

One rubber band is slipped over the ends of each pair of lams. The rubber band should be snug enough to hold the two lams close together but stretchy enough to allow them to separate when the harness involved is supposed to rise. When all the rubber bands are in place, any jack tie-up can be done on the lower lams, using the same length of cord previously used to tie the lower lams for counter march.

The result is a loom that has the flexibility of a jack loom and the harness action of a counter march. Only the harnesses that will rise are tied-up and more than one treadle can be depressed at once. Referring to the earlier example of a four harness fiber construction using tabby and variations of two layers, a skeleton tie-up will suffice (Figure 22). All the combinations necessary can be obtained by depressing groups of treadles, a situation that is impossible with a standard counter march tie-up.

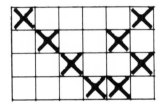

22. Skeleton tie-up

There are three drawbacks to this process. First, the treadles rise higher because of the tension holding the lower lams up. Second, the treadling feels springy. Finally, the rubber bands wear out about every 15 yards. For these reasons this odd process is recommended as a last resort or for experimentation and not for long runs of consistent yard goods where the original counter march tie-up is satisfactory. Of course, once a desired treadling is obtained or the multilayer piece is completed, the change back to counter march is as easy as removing the rubber bands and adding the upper lam ties.

Loom Maintenance

Careful loom maintenance extends the life of the loom. Hardwoods should be cleaned and waxed or oiled regularly, especially in dry or changeable climates. At the same time, lubricate the metal parts of the loom using a cloth saturated with household or sewing machine oil, a spray can of lubricant or a nonstick pan coating such as Pam.

All screws and bolts should be tightened regularly. Waiting until the loom starts to shake and wobble does permanent damage to the joints of the loom by slowly crushing wood, enlarging bolt holes and stripping screws.

Powdered pumice, available from the drug store, and a stiff scrub brush quickly clean and strip the rust off of neglected reeds. Finish the job with an oily cloth or a preserving spray of a nonstick pan coating. In a damp climate, the extra cost of nonrusting reeds rewards the weaver with years of clean service.

Protect the cloth aprons of a loom from excess wear by allotting two rods for each apron instead of one. Pass the first rod through the apron in the usual manner. Using a lightweight loom tying cord, lash the second rod to the first, starting with a knot around the end of the first rod. Pass the lashing cord alternately around the second rod and through the apron slots. Leaving about 2" between the parallel rods, finish the job by tying the lashing cord to the other end of the first rod (Figure 23). The warp threads can now pass around the second rod and between the lashings instead of through the slots in the apron. Another advantage of this technique becomes apparent when the warp is removed from the apron by simply sliding the second rod out of the warp knots and lashings.

A coating of beeswax protects loom tie cords from fraying and drying out while, at the same time, increases the cord's manageability. Beeswax also protects metal heddles from rust and allows them to move freely on the frame.

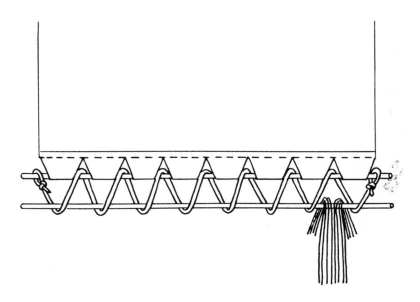

23. Second rod lashed to apron

Improvisations

The old saw that necessity is the mother of invention should have been said first about a weaver, for improvisation seems to be the weaver's forte. Fascinating and useful loom modifications are generated from household miscellany. One of the simplest substitutions for a basic loom part is an extra pickup harness made of a ¼" dowel and jumbo paper clips. The paper clips slide on the dowel and selected warp threads are slipped into the individual clips (Figure 24). This penny-wise harness can also be the basis for a child's loom.

On a slightly larger scale, if a double beam is not available to weave a piece that requires one, a supplementary beam can be made out of two pieces of lumber (1" × 2" or 2" × 4") cut to the length of the existing loom's back beam, a dowel or curtain rod of the same length and some strong loom tying cord.

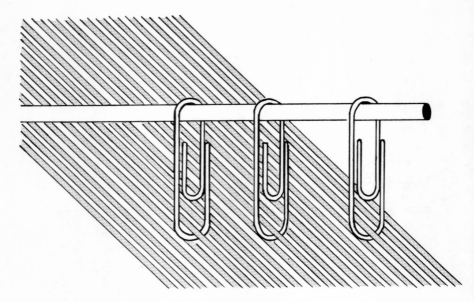

24. Pickup harness

The rod or dowel is attached to a wide side of one piece of lumber using the strong cord and carpet tacks. Starting with an overhand knot tacked to one end of the wide side of the lumber, the cord goes from the lumber, around the dowel and back to the lumber, where it is tacked. This process is repeated every 6″ to 10″, ending with an overhand knot and a tack at the other end of the side of the lumber. The distance from the lumber to the dowel should be long enough to allow the end of the warp to travel from the lumber (which will be secured to the loom below the regular warp beam) to just behind the heddles.

The supplementary warp is wound onto the lumber in as normal a fashion as possible. To do this, put lease sticks in the warp cross. Slip the warp end loops onto the dowel in sections of 6″ to 10″, alternating the groups of warp ends with the cords from the lumber beams. Working on a table, spread the warp in a raddle secured to one edge of the table (Figure 25).

Carefully roll the warp onto the lumber, advancing the lease sticks and using sticks, paper or cardboard strips to keep the warp layers separate and even. Since the supplementary warp beam will be below the loom warp beam, leave at least one yard of the warp unwound.

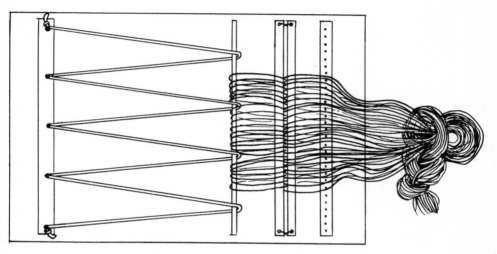

25. Cord and lumber assembly

Next, sandwich the second piece of lumber to the lumber beam using cords tied tightly around the ends of the lumber to keep the lumber beam from rotating and the warp from unwinding (Figure 26).

Temporarily tie the warp sandwich to the back beam of a previously warped loom. Bring the lease sticks and warp into position behind the heddles. Thread, sley and tie-on the warp from both the loom warp beam and the supplementary lumber warp beam.

With the warp ends threaded and secured, drop the warp and lumber sandwich over the back of the loom and tension the supplementary warp by tying the ends of the exposed piece of lumber to the bottom of the loom with heavy cord.

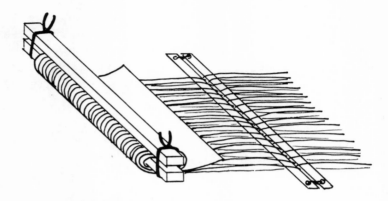

26. Supplementary warp assembly

Alternatively, tension can be applied by hanging weights, such as bleach bottles filled with sand, from the ends of the exposed piece of lumber (Figure 27).

To advance the supplementary warp, loosen the ties holding the sandwich together and unwind some warp. Retie the sandwich and adjust the tension of both warps.

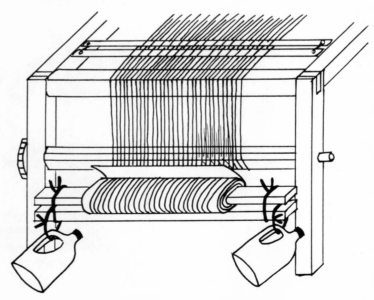

27. Supplementary warp tension

Other Studio Equipment

Warping Boards, Spool Racks and Shuttles

Although the loom is the main tool in a weaving studio, a warping board and spool rack are almost as important. Fortunately, these smaller implements are easier to improvise. Hardwood blocks with upright dowel pegs can be C-clamped to a table forming a makeshift warping board. Ladder-back chairs can act as a warping device as well as a swift and a spool rack with the addition of dowels (Figure 28).

Warping boards, spool racks and even warping mills make interesting wood-working projects. The equipment in Figure 29 can be made out of clear pine, but really should be made of harder wood such as maple or cherry.

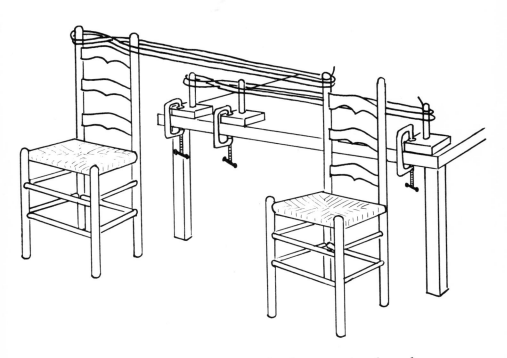

28. Ladder back chairs and other warping boards

29. Warping reel and spool rack plans

Scale: 1 square = 2″

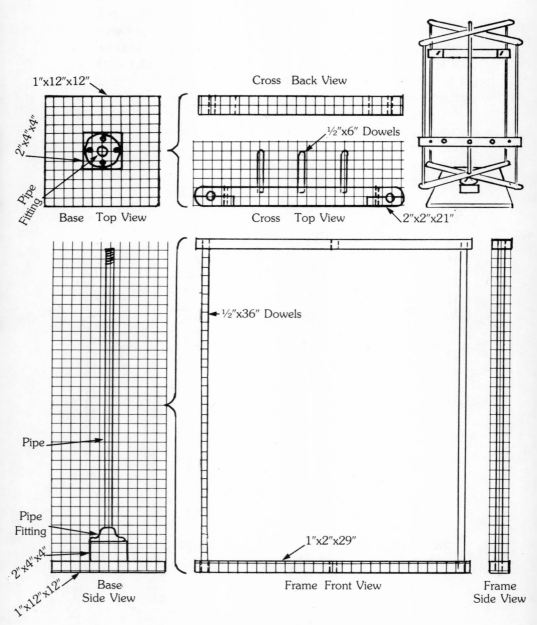

1″x12″x12″

2″x4″x4″

Pipe Fitting

Base Top View

Cross Back View

½″x6″ Dowels

Cross Top View

2″x2″x21″

Pipe

Pipe Fitting

2″x4″x4″

1″x12″x12″

Base Side View

½″x36″ Dowels

1″x2″x29″

Frame Front View

Frame Side View

WARP MILL

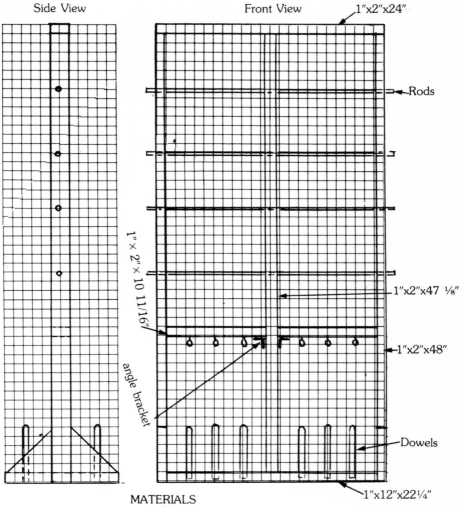

Side View

Front View

1"x2"x24"

Rods

$1" \times 2" \times 10\ 11/16"$

angle bracket

1"x2"x47 1/8"

1"x2"x48"

Dowels

1"x12"x22¼"

MATERIALS

Warp Mill

wood:
5—½" × 36" dowels
4—1" × 2" × 29"
2—2" × 2" × 21"
1—2" × 4" × 4"

metal:
1—½" × 39" pipe and fitting
4—¼" × 2¼" wing nuts
3—washers for pipe
8—wood screws
4—rubber feet

Spool and Cone Rack

wood:
2—1" × 2" × 48"
1—1" × 2" × 47⅛"
1—1" × 2" × 24"
2—1" × 2" × 10-11/16"
1—½" × 36" dowel
1—1" × 12" × 22¼"
    scrap for braces

metal:
6—screw eyes
20—wood screws
2—small angle brackets
4—3/16" × 26" rods

43

SPOOL AND CONE RACK

A pull up from a wall hanger rack, mounted just to the upper right of a warping board, acts as a cone rack. The cones are arranged on the floor below the rack and the warp yarns are drawn from the cones, through the hanger slots, and onto the warp board. The nearest slot is reserved for a bundle of cotton thrums used to tie the warp (Figure 30).

Every weaver likes lots of shuttles and, depending on the weaving variety, the selection should include all kinds—from slender boat shuttles to large rug shuttles. The large flat shuttles, sometimes called rag or rug shuttles, and ski shuttles are used for heavy yarns, while boat shuttles are best for weaving yardage, lightweight wall hangings and linens.

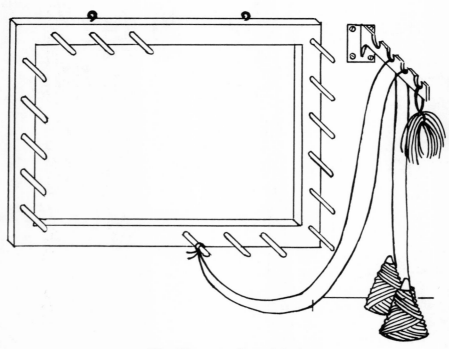

30. Warping board helper

Purchased Accessories and Household Helpers

With the boat shuttle comes the need for bobbins, a bobbin-winder and paper quills. The Swedish hand bobbin-winder is satisfactory, but weavers with access to a machine shop can adapt an old-fashioned sewing machine bobbin-winder by attaching a longer shaft to the bobbin-winding wheel (Figure 31).

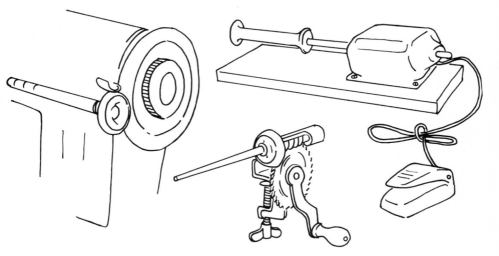

31. Bobbin winders

The cardboard tubes on the bottom edge of dry cleaner's hangers can be cut into sections and used as quills. Crisp paper cut into 3" or 4" squares can be wound around a pencil to form a quill (Figure 32).

An inexpensive and time-saving ball-winder saves lots of hand winding and prepares yarn for warping or convenient storage (Figure 33). Balls of coarse yarn should be secured with the outside thread, removed from the ball winder and used from the center of the ball. Balls of fine or slippery yarn should be left on the ball-winding cone and used from the outside to avoid tangles.

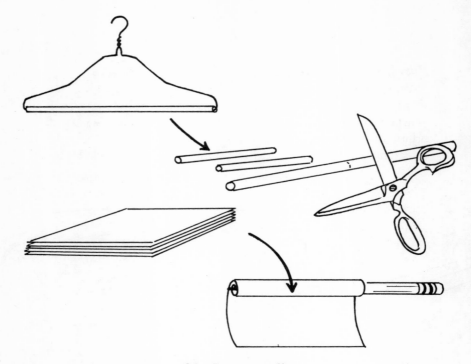

32. Paper quills

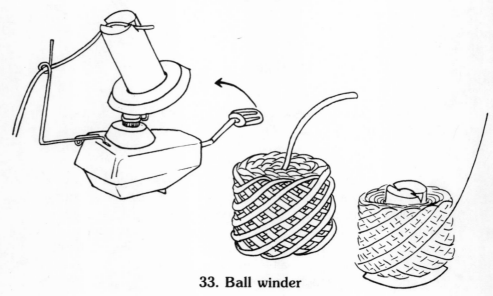

33. Ball winder

Every facet of weaving is replete with its own gadgets. As just one example, several clever tools assist the weaver with the pile rug process. The flossa rod and the flossa knife allow the weaver to make rugs with rows of equal length pile using a continuous weft yarn. Various sizes of flossa rods are available to make short or deep pile rugs or wall hangings. Flossa scissors, which have curved blades, cut the pile without clipping the warp threads and can be used for other clipped surfaces such as corduroy. For those who like a shaggier surface but get tired of cutting the lengths of yarn for the knots, an adjustable yarn-cutter measures and cuts 2¼", 3½" or 4½" lengths while all you do is turn the crank (Figure 34).

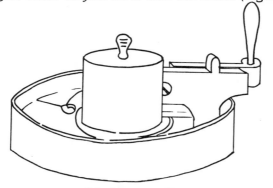

34. Yarn cutter

When it comes to weaving tools, ingenious improvisations abound. Mexican weavers manipulate an umbrella spoke like a long needle to get the ultimate weft shot in their blankets, which are made with selvedge edges on all four sides. This idea could easily be adapted to any weaving situation where the last few shots are a tight squeeze.

Judging from the nature of many weaving tool improvisations, weavers must spend a lot of time in the kitchen. Forks double as tapestry combs and vegetable brushes are used to tease napped fabric. Styrofoam meat trays are cut into small flat shuttles and nonstick sprays are used to lubricate looms.

47

Stick-on cup hooks attached to the castle hold scissors and tape measure.

Bricks and encyclopedias are favored as weights to pile around the feet of a "walking" loom, while used bleach bottles containing measured amounts of sand are perfect hanging weights.

Stocking a Tool Box

A weaver actually needs two kinds of tool boxes: one for tools to fix equipment and another akin to a sewing basket. The one that resembles a sewing basket should contain all the sundries needed in the weaving process, including straight pins, tapestry needles, sewing needles, crochet hooks, reed hooks, thread-snipping scissors and tailor's scissors, tape measure, masking tape and fabric glue.

The regular tool box is most often neglected. This tool box should contain wrenches and screwdrivers that fit the loom, tack hammer and upholstery tacks to keep the apron attached, wire cutters to remove a pair of crossed metal heddles, and pliers to straighten out cotter pins and to repair friction brakes. Beeswax; furniture polish for the loom, and Elmer's glue all come in handy.

Chapter 2:

Fibers

The enjoyment of weaving, both in process and in use, depends on the fibers and yarns employed. The proper yarn for a particular weaving works easily, produces the desired surface and withstands the intended use.

In Search of the Right Yarn

The yarn search is, in itself, a fascinating preoccupation. Between local weaving shops, mail order suppliers, commercial conference exhibits and other weavers, the sources for buying and trading are nearly endless. Each source, in turn, presents a varied array of materials and prices. In order to make enlightened selections, some knowledge of the various fibers becomes necessary.

Wool

Wool has two basic forms for weaving: worsted and woolen (or homespun). Worsted, a light-weight long-staple yarn that is sometimes mercerized, is used for baby blankets, scarves and dress fabrics. Homespun or woolen is a denser, rougher material and is used for tweeds, overshot, upholstery and decorative pieces. Wool roving is sometimes used in wall hangings to add texture and depth.

Woolens use their own system for determining the size of various yarns. This system is based on a *cut* that has 300 yards in a pound where a 10 cut has ten times as many yards in a pound. After supplying the ply as denominator, simple arithmetic yields the number of yards in a pound. For example a 10 cut, 2 ply yarn (10/2) = (10 × 300)/2 = 1,500 yards. Occassionally, fine wool yarn may be put up in *runs,* where a single run has 1,600 yards to a pound and a 5 run has 8,000 to a pound.

Worsted is identified by counts of 560 yards in a pound. The more counts, the more yards, with 10 count worsted having 5,600 yards in a pound.

Wools benefit from storage in skeins, since the constant tension on a spool may ruin the elasticity of wool yarn. For the same reason, you should weave wool warps as soon as possible and release the loom tension when not actually weaving.

Reduce the annoying warp breakage incurred in the weaving of fine, hard-spun wools by dampening the wool on the loom during the weaving process and thus increasing warp elasticity and flexibility. In *The Shuttlecraft Book of American Handweaving,* Mary Atwater describes the process as follows. Dampen the warp behind the heddles with a sponge just before advancing the warp, and dampen it again after the warp is advanced. Lay a damp towel over the back of the loom while the weaving is in progress.

While the same worsted can be used for both warp and weft, warp and weft woolens are often different yarns. The woolen warp yarn is usually a hard twist yarn with a Z, or right hand, twist. The weft yarn is slightly loftier and is an S, or left hand, twist (Figure 35). Although a warp yarn can be used as a weft in a twill, a weft yarn cannot be used as a warp yarn because it is too weak. Nor can a hard-spun warp yarn be used in a plain weave with the same warp without risking a crepe effect caused by all the Z twists.

Last but not least, the gentle cycle of a washing machine, mild soap and lukewarm water can be used to wash woolen yardage. This initial washing is important to full, or finish, the cloth. Worsted wools that will be dry-cleaned in use can be professionally cleaned and steamed to finish them.

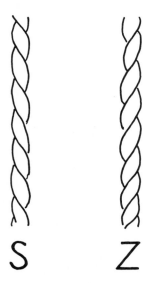

35. S and Z twist

Wool tapestry should be blocked. Steaming on a flat surface from the wrong side with an iron and damp cloth will suffice to block most pieces, but a more drastic system is necessary if the piece is anything but flat and square. First, temporarily sew rug binding around all the edge using carpet thread and a canvas needle. Pulling the tapestry into a square, tack the rug binding down to a clean, flat surface away from direct heat and light. Dampen the whole piece by covering it with a wet sheet and then allow the sheet and weaving to dry naturally.

51

Cotton

Cotton is an easy fiber to use. It is smooth and strong, soft to the touch, loftier than linen, absorbent and easy to launder. Long-staple plied cottons make trouble-free warps.

Cotton is traditionally used with wool in overshot or summer and winter for coverlets, and with some reservations*, in bags, pillow tops and upholstery. Cotton's absorbent qualities make it ideal for ikat or jaspé and good for household "linens" and clothing. Cotton rug and tapestry warps are durable and inexpensive choices. As floss, cotton shimmers in small overshot and band weavings while, as bulky roving and slub yarns, it adds quickly-woven texture to pillows and wall hangings. However, avoid using cotton roving as rug weft or pile; even if the weft is nearly concealed, the soft cotton can't stand up to hard use.

Cottons, also, use their own system for determining the size of various yarns, but the size/ply arithmetic remains the same as for wool. Number 1 cotton has 840 yards to the pound and, as the numbers increase, the number of yards in a pound also increases. For example, a number 20, 2 ply (20/2) = (840 × 20)/2 = 8,400 yards in a pound.

The origin of a pound of number 1 cotton equaling 840 yards is complex but interesting. It seems the circumference of a reel was 1½ yards or one thread. There are eighty threads in one skein or 120 yards. Seven skeins made up a hank of 840 yards and the number of hanks in a pound was *the* number.

Avoid uninterrupted expanses of tabby when using plain, plied cotton, since the lack of texture and luster is monotonous. Also avoid mixing cotton with linen. Not only does cotton detract from the natural texture and luster of linen, but cotton doesn't blend with rayon the way linen does.

White or natural cottons can be washed in hot water with a cold rinse, while colored cottons can be washed in warm water using the gentle cycle of the washing machine.

---

* Long overshots should be avoided in fabrics that receive heavy wear.

Linen

Three types of linen yarn are commonly used in weaving: plied (or round), singles (or line) and floss. Linen is measured in *leas* in a manner similar to woolen and cotton yarns. A single of 1 lea has 300 yards in a pound, and the more leas, the more yards. For example a 20 lea, 3 ply = $(20 \times 300)/3 = 2,000$ yards in a pound.

Select 50/50 weaves such as damask, double face twill, huck, lace, M's and O's and tabby. Overshot, crackle, and summer and winter should be avoided except as borders in linen weaving.

Like some wools, fine plied linen may be dampened on the loom to facilitate weaving. This dampening helps the cloth to merge together by softening the fibers.

A good warp dressing for difficult wool or linen is made from flax seed and water. The seed and water are boiled and the seeds are strained out. Then the resulting syrup is watered down to the consistency of thin starch. Warps can be dipped in dressing and wound on the loom while slightly damp.

Fabric that is 100% linen can look as rough and stiff as burlap when it comes off the loom. The lustrous, supple nature of linen results from proper finishing. Of course all repairs should be made first, along with any hemstitching or knotting. After checking the fibers for colorfastness, launder the material in the washing machine using hot water and a normal cycle. Remove the material from the washer, roll it up and place the roll in a plastic bag. Now for the shock-treatment that transforms the cloth: pop the bagged cloth into the freezer. As the freezing expands the water trapped in the cloth, the ice crystals break down the harsh fibers of the linen. When the cloth is completely frozen, remove it from the freezer and press it dry with a hot iron.

Other Materials

Although wool, cotton and linen are the "big three" of weaving materials, silk is certainly the most sumptuous. As lustrous plied filaments or the softly elegant tussah and raw silks, this fiber yields elegant yardage, sensuous wall hangings, even Chinese carpets. But silk shares a flaw with another common fiber, jute. Both are susceptible to the effects of sunlight and rot. Stains, exposed folds and direct sunlight can very quickly ruin fine silk.

Silk and other filament yarns are measured by *deniers,* with the size of the yarn increasing with the denier number. Thus, 1 denier rayon has 4,465,513 yards in a pound and 100 denier rayon has 44,645 yards in a pound. These odd numbers are based on 1 denier having 450 meters in .05 grams.

Sisal is a rough, strong fiber that is gaining in appeal because it is inexpensive, accepts dyes and is more durable than jute. Due to its stiffness, sisal is best woven wet.

The natural fiber family includes a linen-like material called ramie which doubles as cotton too. Raffia is also available as a weaving fiber of limited use. Reeds used in Roman shades are also woven wet.

The synthetics form a world of their own. They range from rayon, a fiber made from cellulose, to a wide range of nylons, acrylics masquerading as wools, and olefins for tough, stain-resistant upholstery.

Even metallics and metals appear in weavings. Metallic yarns are usually coated Mylar and, although they are heat sensitive, weave easily as weft. Metal wires, however, should be treated with a plastic film to prevent tarnishing when they are incorporated in weavings.

Luxurious fur scraps, available from furriers for a song or, less desirably, from old fur coats, present some unusual handling problems. Fur should be cut from the back (leather side) of the pelt with an Exacto knife or single-edged razor blade. For the best results, a cutting plan should be designed that considers both the shape of the pelt for maximum use and the direction of the growth of the hair. Usually the nap of the fur runs up to down in a garment. The reverse direction yields a less lustrous, fuzzier appearance. Naps that run side to side give the appearance of cowlicks.

54

Dull, brittle or smelly fur should be discarded. However, fur can be cleaned with several preparations including dry shampoo, pet foam shampoo or corn meal. Any of these should be worked in, allowed to collect grime, and brushed out with a vegetable brush.

Mix and Match

It's often necessary to mix yarns from different companies to obtain a desired surface or color scheme. Of course, the selected yarns should be compatible materials that, at least, share the same cleaning process. For consistent surface and selvedges, the yarns ought to be tested for necessary similarities of size, stretch, spin and luster.

To compare two yarns for equal diameter, cut 16" lengths of the yarns to be compared, fold the lengths in half and link the folded yarns together. Twist the yarns between your fingers until a uniform cord of four strands of each material develops. Pull the cord between the thumb and forefinger to feel any difference between the yarns (Figure 36).

Any difference in diameter makes noticeable textural changes in the cloth and causes weft pattern units to expand and contract as the yarns are varied. Differences in warp yarn diameter cause take up at an uneven rate, producing cloth with ridges and puckers (Figure 37).

The same undesirable result occurs when yarns of different elasticity are mixed in either warp or weft. To test yarns for elasticity cut 36" of each material to be tested while the yarns are not under tension. Then stretch each yarn to its maximum extension and compare the results.

Certain interesting results can be obtained by purposely combining a variety of yarns in one piece. However, the piece should be planned to exploit this puckering feature and long lengths of such a fabric may become difficult to weave as the warp tension becomes more and more uneven. Such effects as seersucker, scalloped edges and ripples, caused by a variety of materials, can be used to design advantage.

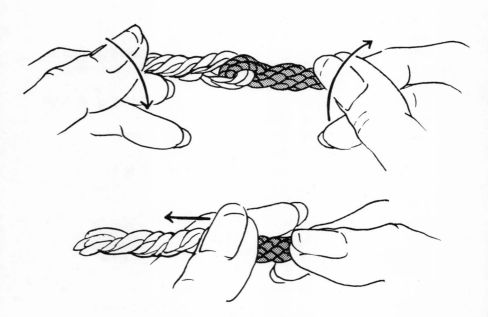

36. Comparing yarn diameters

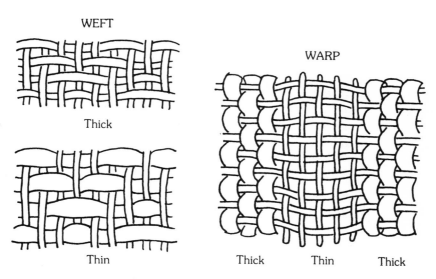

WEFT

WARP

Thick

Thin

Thick   Thin   Thick

37. Mixing yarn diameters

Mystery Materials

When the fiber content is not listed on an odd lot of yarn or the content label is lost, simple tests can be used to determine the general nature of the fiber in question. Common methods include the chemical reactions of burning a strand of the yarn or soaking another strand in a lye solution.

The results of these two tests indicate the fiber content of an unidentified yarn. Burning wool and other animal fibers smell terrible—like burning hair—and leave some residue. Many man-made fibers melt rather than burn and smell equally bad—like plastics and chemicals. Vegetable fibers burn with little unpleasant smell and leave a soft powdery ash. Lye will dissolve wool but it only softens linen and usually doesn't affect synthetics.

Will It Warp?

A wide range of possibilities for warp materials is opened to the weaver who uses some tricks for controlling warp breakage on the loom. However, it is best to check warp materials prior to use for strength and durability. First, a yarn used as a warp should contain long filaments with sufficient spin to keep the fiber from disintegrating as the reed moves around it. The yarn should also be free of unsupported slubs that might pull the yarn apart in the heddles or reed. To test for warp suitability, pull the yarn in question back and forth between the thumb and index finger several times then snap the yarn gently and repeatedly. If the yarn remains intact during these tests, it will probably work as warp (Figure 38).

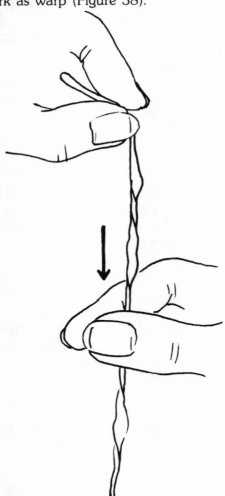

38. Test warp yarns

Of course not all yarns that pass this test are suitable for the warp. Spun fiberglass loses its tensile strength under prolonged tension and, more important, endangers the weaver's health. Other fibers, such as mohair with a nylon core, are strong enough to warp but present sticky problems when a shed is attempted.

Many fibers that might warp well are too weak to make a good selvedge edge. If four stronger threads, of a similar fiber content and elasticity, are warped at both edges, smooth strong selvedges will result. If the intended use of the fabric is yardage, the color of these four stronger threads is unimportant since they will be cut away or hidden in seams. It is most important that all warp threads stretch the same.

Handling Yarns

Skeined Yarns

Skeined yarns present serious tangling problems if they are not carefully handled. Skeins should be tied loosely in several locations to preserve the order of the reel in the yarn.

To secure a skein for storage, hold the skein on both hands, twist the skein, then push one end through the opposite opening (Figure 39). The skein will untwist on itself thus securing loose threads that might otherwise tangle.

With patience, untangling a neglected skein is usually possible. Handle the skein as little as possible until the extent of the tangle is understood. Place as many original loops as possible on a skein winder and begin a ball. Don't pull on the yarn; instead gently pat it when a tangle is reached. For severe tangles pluck the threads like guitar strings and pass the ball through the appropriate spaces in the tangle. Keep the balls small to maintain their maneuverability. For hopeless tangles, cut the skein to make needlework lengths, rya knots or inlay lengths.

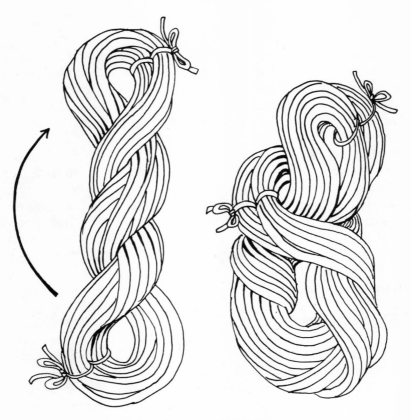

39. Securing a skein

Balls

Skeins of yarn can be used directly, but they are most commonly wound into balls by using a swift and ball winder.

If you don't have a ball winder, start a center-pull ball by hand-winding a figure eight butterfly around the thumb and little finger of one hand. Remove the butterfly and secure its loops by winding the continuing yarn around the butterfly until all but the ends of the butterfly are covered. Continue to wind the ball always leaving the pull-string exposed. Finish the ball by securing the end of the yarn under the last winding (Figure 40).

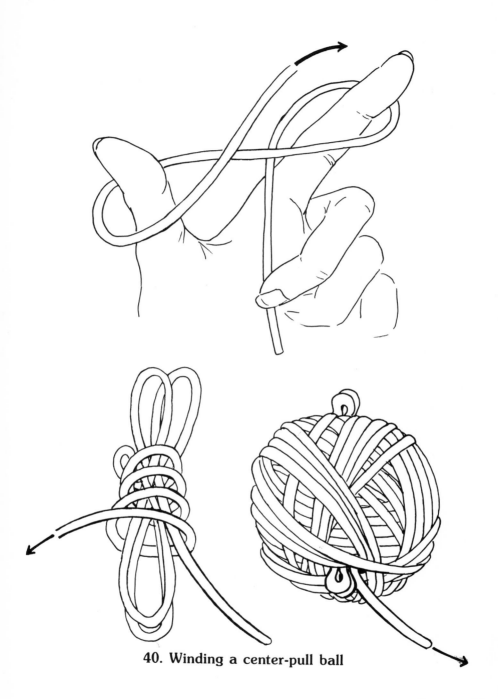

40. Winding a center-pull ball

Keep noncenter-pull balls of yarn from rolling around by placing each one in a small, crisp paper-bag. Cylindrical ice cream cartons with snug lids can also be used to control big balls by punching a hole in the lid and feeding the yarn out through the hole (Figure 41).

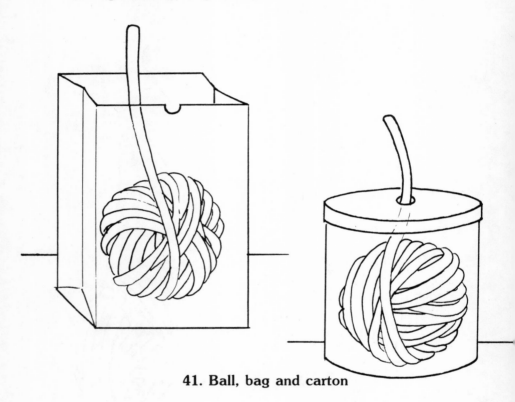

41. Ball, bag and carton

Cones
Remove yarn from cones by drawing the yarn straight up through an eye hook directly above the cone which is placed on a vertical peg (Figure 42). Spools of yarn should be placed on a horizontal rack so that the yarn can be removed by rotating the spool.

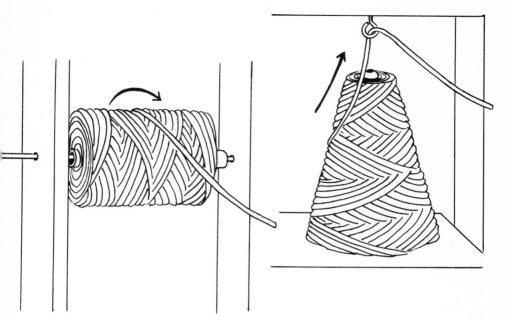

42. Spool and cone on rack

When a single cone is being combined with spools on a horizontal-rod spool-rack, the resulting catching and flopping of the cone on the rod is avoided by making a cone adaptor out of a large and a small sewing thread spool (preferably wooden). Using a rasp, trim the flange off one end of each spool and glue the unflanged end of the large spool to the flanged end of the small spool, carefully lining up the center holes. When it's dry, push the adaptor into the cone, small end first, until the adaptor is wedged into the narrow end of the cone. Then place the adapted cone on a spool rack for use along with spools (Figure 43).

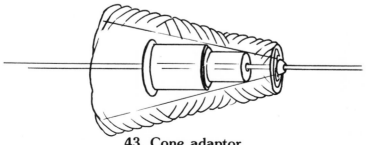

43. Cone adaptor

63

The ice cream carton mentioned earlier also allows two coned yarns to be used as one by stacking the cones. The first cone is placed in the container and its yarn is threaded out through the hole in the lid and up through the second cone. The second cone is placed over the hole in the lid of the closed carton and both yarns are worked from the second cone (Figure 44).

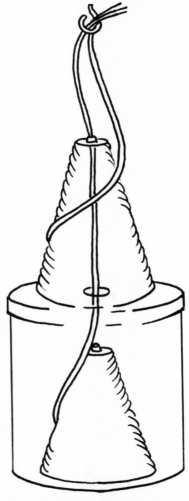

44. Cones and carton

Bobbins

Bobbin winding is an art and, as with other such endeavors, there is more than one style. Plastic bobbins are easiest to fill because the weft yarn can't fall off the edges. Paper quills are inexpensive and, with a little practice, easy to fill.

The most common mistake of bobbin winding is overfilling the quill. Yarn on the bobbin should never touch the shuttle wall, nor should yarn touch the ends of a quill.

Of the two methods of filling a quill, one is definitely easier to master while the other may be better for fine yarns. In the first method, the yarn is guided from side to side while turning the bobbin winder and each layer of yarn created is narrower than the one before it. Method two involves making humps of yarn at each side of the quill and then filling in the valley; the weft must not go over the humps of yarn or the quill won't work. Passing the yarn through an extra eye hook or two controls bouncy yarns while heavy yarns can be wound directly on bobbins.

Bobbin winding reveals an interesting difference between cone and spool put-up. The yarn coming up off an upright cone has an added twist, while the spooled yarn comes off straight. Therefore, yarns that kink or back-spin from an upright cone should be transferred to a spool rack by using a cone adaptor (Figure 45).

Paired bobbin threads that unwind unevenly cause real weaving troubles; after every few shots the weaver must deal with dropping weft thread. The reason for this trouble is usually the combination of dissimilar yarns: for example, a smooth and a rough yarn, or a spool put-up combined with cones or balls. The solution is to apply tension to the loose yarn with your fingers while winding the bobbin. Control both yarn tensions by closing your fingers around the yarn (Figure 46).

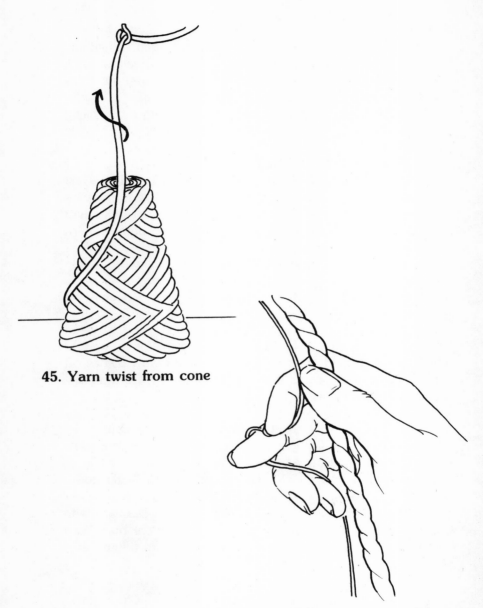

45. Yarn twist from cone

46. Controlling two bobbin yarns

Using Leftovers

No matter how well planned a weaving is, there are always leftovers—maybe a little yarn on a cone or some bobbins and, of course, the thrums from the loom.

Thrifty weavers find other functions for thrums and leftovers. Full bobbins and put-up leftovers become accent colors for other weavings. Smooth, strong yarn thrums, particularly cottons, can be used to tie and prepare warps. Hard-twist wools make rya knots and even small scraps can work in tassels and pom-poms.

Twice-woven weavings use thrums and scraps to make marvelously decorative chenilles, rag rugs and bristly doormats. These pieces soak up pounds of scrap yarn and fabric. Literally rags to riches pieces, twice-woven weavings, in their simplest forms, involve cutting cloth (purchased, hand woven or rags) into strips for weft. More complex twice-woven weavings are actually thrice-woven when strips of cloth as well as yarns are used as weft for making chenille yarn, which is destined to be weft in yet another step in the process.

Weaving chenille yarn is an interesting endeavor. Chenille yarns come in all sizes and materials but the basic idea is always the same. The loom is dressed with groups of four to eight ends threaded tabby and set very close, with a skip of a few dents to several inches between groups. Selvedges are added to control the outside fluff of the edge chenille strips.

Although almost any materials can be included in chenille yarn, considering some simple constraints and variables results in easier weaving and a more durable chenille yarn. The material for the warp should be strong and smooth enough to endure the friction of treadling tabby with a close sett, but with enough tooth to hold the chenille weft in place. The weft also needs a little tooth plus some loft to form the fluffy part of the chenille yarn.

The spaces between the warp groups can, of course, vary according to the desires of the weaver, the limits being determined by the material. Very fine yarns form rather stringy chenille yarn when the space between the warp groups is very large. Thick, firm yarns, with very little loft, need a large space between the warp groups to keep the materials secure and to maintain pleasing proportions.

The following sample chenille yarn can be made from a wide range of materials.

Warp: 12/2 cotton
Reed: 15 dent
Sett: 8 ends, 2 per dent, skip 22 dents between repeats
Threading: tabby
Selvedge treatment: 4 ends, 2 per dent, skip 15 dents. The warp length and width, number of groups and weft are all up to the weaver.
Weaving directions: weave in a variety of thrums either as individual strands or in groups. Each strand need not go all the way across the warp. In fact, good color effects are achieved by laying in small lengths of colored yarns. Before the web winds on to the cloth beam, cut the weft between the groups of warp (Figure 47).
Finishing: trim away the selvedges. Tie the ends of each group of warps into an overhand knot.

The resulting chenille yarn is then ready to be used as weft for another warp of the weaver's choice. The chenille yarn can be planned to produce the color, texture, and pattern of this second or twice-woven piece. Chenille yarns of various diameters can be woven from the same warp by varying the width of the space between the warp groups. Color mixtures and changes can be made in the chenille yarn's weft; the resulting multicolored chenille yarns are then woven into a twice-woven piece. Handsome hombre effects result from a series of planned weft color progressions in the chenille yarn's weft where the length of this color progression is not equal to the width of the intended twice-woven piece (Figure 48).

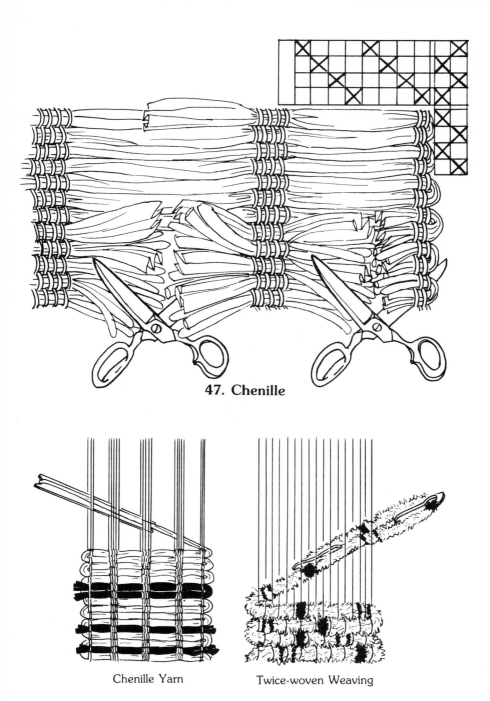

47. Chenille

Chenille Yarn   Twice-woven Weaving

48. Hombre chenille

69

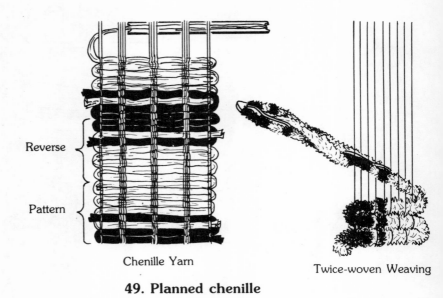

Reverse

Pattern

Chenille Yarn

Twice-woven Weaving

49. Planned chenille

The most challenging situation is to completely control the design created by the chenille weft in the twice-woven piece by planning exactly where the colors will fall in the chenille yarn. The width of the twice-woven piece, plus an allowance for a 10% weft takeup, determines the length of the corresponding chenille yarn's designed weft pattern. To weave more than one pattern on the warp used to make the chenille yarn (thus producing a longer chenille yarn length), reverse the pattern sequences each time a pattern unit is completed (Figure 49).

Chapter 3:

Designing and Planning

Creative Drafting

Drafting is an integral part of the weaving process. Using a specialized diagrammatic form, drafting indicates how the loom and weaver control the interlacement of threads. In a weaving draft, the horizontal lines indicate the threading of the harnesses. The intersection of the vertical and horizontal grids shows the tie-up of treadles and harnesses, and the vertical graph contains the treadling sequence (Figure 50). Learning to draft will amply reward the weaver with unlimited weaves and variations.

Threading drafts can be right- or left-handed. Some are written and read right to left, while other drafts, with no other significant differences, are read vice-versa. The key to the threading direction is the tie-up block where the drafts usually begin. Other indications of the draft's beginning are selvedge and border placement as well as directional arrows, vertical double lines or a bar. Sometimes the threading marks are in the spaces and sometimes they cross the lines, especially in Scandinavian drafts. Some weavers draft with numbers and others like to indicate colors, contributing to the many draft variations (Figure 51).

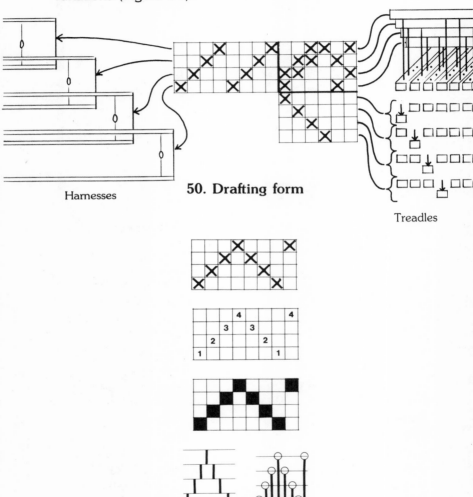

Harnesses

50. Drafting form

Treadles

51. Various drafts of the same threading

Treadlings are usually given in an abbreviated form that shows only the pattern, assuming the use of tabby after each pattern shot. Another common convenience is the use of numbers to indicate the repetition of a pattern block (Figure 52). Frequently the treadling and tie-up are omitted from colonial overshot patterns. A standard tie-up is assumed and the treadling is developed by squaring the four block, four harness threading (see Blocks). A standard four harness tie-up differs from a skeleton (one harness to one treadle) tie-up in that two harnesses are tied to each treadle. Harnesses one and two are tied to the first treadle. Harnesses two and three are

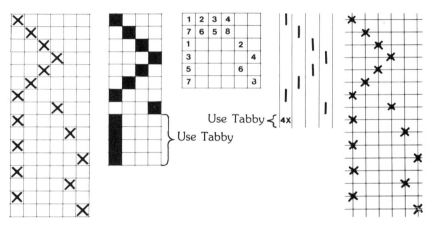

52. Various drafts of the same treadling

tied to the second treadle. Harnesses three and four are tied to the third treadle. The pattern-treadling combinations are completed by tying harnesses four and one to the fourth treadle. Finally, harnesses one and three are tied to the fifth treadle and harnesses two and four to the sixth treadle, creating the tabby for most weaves.

One of the easiest changes to make in a draft is the tie-up change from rising to sinking shed. To accomplish this, simply tie-up the harnesses *not* indicated by the rising shed tie-up.

Occasionally both tie-ups are given with the rising and sinking sheds marked with different symbols (Figure 53).

The weaving draft is a graphed picture of the cloth structure, with vertical columns of squares representing warp ends and horizontal rows representing the weft. Marked squares may represent the rising warp threads while blank squares represent the weft. Again, as with the threading draft, this arrangement is merely a convention (Figure 54). The weaving draft is necessary to check a newly-drawn threading draft in the analysis of cloth.

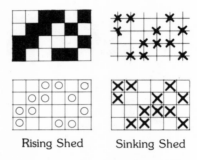

Rising Shed   Sinking Shed

53. Various tie-up drafts

54. Weaving draft

Cloth Analysis

It would be a lie to say that cloth analysis is immediately, creatively stimulating. It is, rather, a time consuming chore whose redeeming grace is that it opens the door to a world of information about cloth design.

Cloth analysis begins with a swatch of intriguing cloth. The first investigation determines which threads are the warp and which are the weft. If the swatch is from a selvedge area, the answer is obvious—the warp is parallel to the selvedge. An unselvedged swatch requires more looking, keeping in mind that weft is loftier and has less twist while warp has less stretch, shows reed marks occasionally and, in production fabrics, may contain stripes.

When the warp direction is determined, begin a weaving draft by taking the swatch apart, one thread at a time, and recording the interlacement of each warp and weft thread (Figure 55).

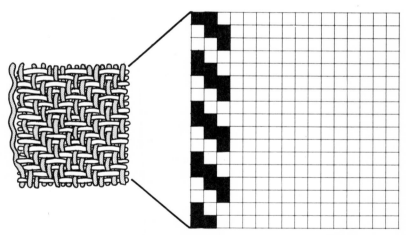

55. Record interlacement of warp and weft

From this weaving draft, a complete draft including thread-ing, tie-up and treadling can be obtained. Starting with a skeleton tie-up, arbitrarily assign the first warp thread to the first harness and record its action by marking the first treadle every time the first warp is raised.

Continue the process by assigning the second warp to the second harness, unless it happens to be moving exactly the same way as the first thread, in which case it also belongs on the first harness. Record the second warp's action with marks in the second treadling column.

The third thread is treated in the same way, except that it is compared with both the one and two warp threads to see if it belongs in either of those harnesses before it is assigned to the third harness (Figure 56).

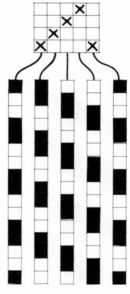

56. Assign warps

The fourth warp is compared to the one, two and three warps before a fourth harness is considered. Each time a warp thread sheds in the same way as a previous thread, it is assigned to that thread's harness. The draft is complete when a full pattern in the cloth has been recorded (Figure 57).

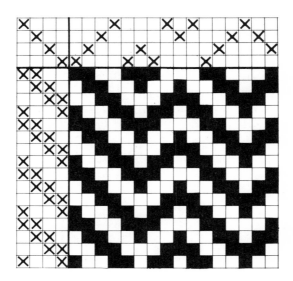

57. Complete draft from swatch

Now the treadling can be simplified by making a new and more complete tie-up. Reading across the treadling, assign the first line of harnesses treadled to the first treadle. Assign the second line of harnesses treadled to the second treadle and so on, until all the necessary combinations are tied-up (Figure 58).

If the threading exhibits an odd-even arrangement of threads throughout the pattern draft, or every other end can otherwise be treadled, a true tabby can be woven.

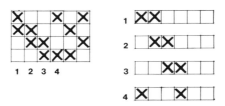

58. Complete tie-up

Twill

Twill weaves and their variations comprise a large portion of weaving drafts. Twilled cloths have more luster, warmth, density and bias than plain-woven goods. Besides the characteristic diagonal weaves, the twill threadings produce tabby, double-faced, tubular, double layer and double width fabrics, as well as satin and ribbed cloth.

Certain secrets assist in the production of fine twilled cloth. For example: setting twill cloth closer than the corresponding plain weave cloth of the same materials allows for the fact that pairs or groups of threads will be working together in each pick. Picks per inch should equal ends per inch in well balanced twills with a resulting 45 degree pattern angle (Figure 59).

59. Twill angle

Additional twill-threaded harnesses not only produce a wider variety of pattern possibilities but actually solve structural problems. Very closely sett plain weaves, worked on six or more twill-threaded harnesses, shows less wear from the friction of the heddles than does the corresponding two- or four-harness weave (Figure 60). For very sticky warps, such as closely sett mohair or slub, the harnesses involved in a given

78

treadling can be lifted one at a time to separate the threads and produce a clean shed. As a rule, never put more than twenty ends per inch on one harness, no matter how fine and strong the material.

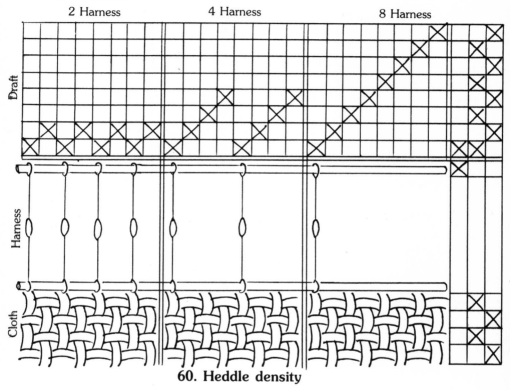

60. Heddle density

Just as wear on a close sett warp is reduced by using more harnesses, it is often better to plan on several ends per dent than to use a very fine reed, which adds to the wear on fragile warp threads. As many as six ends can be put in one dent; resulting reed marks usually come out in the wash. Thus, thirty ends per inch sleyed three per dent in a ten dent reed may fare better than the same warp sleyed two per dent in a fifteen dent reed.

It should also be noted that the shaft nearest the shed should hold the most threads, since its shed is naturally the deepest (Figure 61).

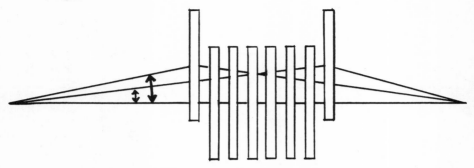

61. Comparison of front and back harnesses

Blocks

The versatile units called blocks embody one of the most powerful drafting concepts. Designed like checkerboards, which alternate dark and light squares, two block drafts are created by grids of intersecting lines. The design possibilities are regulated by the arrangement of grid lines and the kind of block threading selected. In the late 1960s, blocks produced familiar and effective "Op" art designs. Traditional block patterns include nostalgic colonial designs and crisp Scandinavian borders.

To create a block design, simply draw one grid of vertical stripes and cross it with a series of horizontal lines to form a second intersecting grid. Fill in every other space created to produce the design effect. By trying different grids, various patterns are developed (Figure 62).

These personalized checkerboards can be translated into any two-block, four-harness weave, including monk's belts, honeycomb, summer and winter, M's and O's, Swedish laces and even reversing twills. Each weave has its own characteristic way of producing the block pattern.

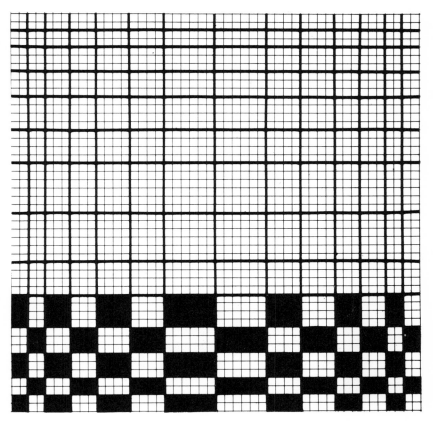

62. Creating a block design grid

Monk's belts is a straightforward block interpretation that works as overshot to produce a clearly contrasting design of floating threads on the surface of the cloth. The minimum pattern unit is two threads in a block, and the width of a pattern block is limited by the nature of overshot weft threads, which tend to catch or droop if the weft thread floating on the surface of the cloth is too long. Thus, a sample monk's belt design contains various numbers of repeats of both block "A" and block "B" (Figure 63).

81

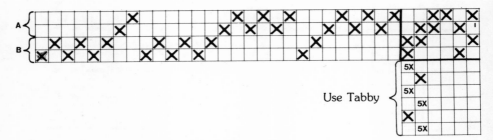

63. Sample monk's belt

Summer and winter is suitable for patterns with large blocks since the pattern threads are tied down by every fourth thread. In this weave a tabby is threaded alternately on the two front harnesses while the remaining harnesses (be there two, six or more) each create one pattern block (Figure 64). The warp and tabby weft should be a contrasting color to the loftier pattern weft.

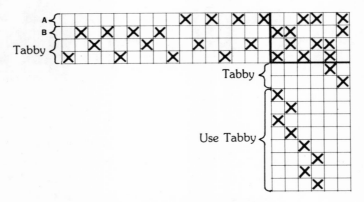

64. Sample summer and winter

M's and O's is a similar but subtler weave, based on collaps-ing, or distorted, warp and weft. The pattern unit is a multiple of eight and can be as wide as desired. However, for the best results, avoid collapsing pattern blocks that consistently fall on the selvedge. Either treadle the opposite blocks more frequently or thread the selvedge threads in a twill. Also, restrict pattern areas to stripes, borders and checks, avoiding a field of collapsing pattern units (Figure 65).

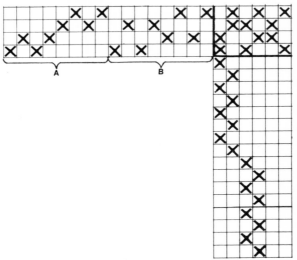

65. Sample M's and O's

Short drafts are super shorthand intended to indicate the length and placement of blocks. These short drafts are particularly applicable to block weaves like summer and winter, where the difference between the blocks is simple to understand and remember. Expand the short draft by substituting a repeat of the appropriate block threading for each indicated square of the short draft (Figure 66).

Four block overshot weaves can be woven on four harness looms because the blocks overlap. Harness one is part of the 1–2 block and 4–1 block. Harness two is paired with both harness one and harness three; harness three also combines with four, producing a total of four pattern combinations: 1–2, 2–3, 3–4 and 4–1.

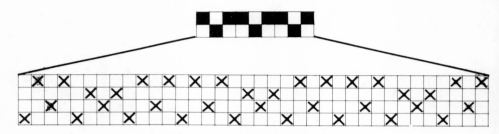

66. Short and long drafts

The occurrence of speckled areas in overshot weavings is the result of overlapping blocks. When harnesses one and two are raised as a block, the harness one threads (that are planned to pair in another shed with harness four) and the harness two threads (that will complete the 2–3 block) create shaded areas along with overshot. These speckled accidentals are usually omitted in the planning and drawing of a new weaving draft to simplify the drafting process.

Overshot blocks may be designed as two sets of opposite pattern blocks: the 1–2 and 3–4 blocks as with monk's belt, or the 1–4 and 2–3 blocks. Rose, star and table motifs are drafted on opposite pattern blocks. Diamond, cross and wheel designs use all four blocks in diagonal arrangements.

Justifying

Overshot patterns that are planned to fit the field they occupy produce the best overall effect. Honeysuckle, for example, contains twenty-six threads per repeat. Thus it only fits perfectly on warps with a multiple of twenty-six threads (actually, twenty-six times the number of repeats plus one thread to finish the last descending twill).

What happens when the warp is planned to be 20″ wide and the best sett for the warp selected is twelve ends per inch? There are obviously twelve times twenty plus four (for selvedge) or 244 ends in the warp. Nine repeats of the honeysuckle pattern are possible for a total of nine times twenty-six or 234 pattern-threaded ends and ten ends remaining.

What happens to these ten ends depends on the desired product. If the piece can be narrower, the solution is to forget the spare ends. Conversely, if the project can be wider, ten repeats can be threaded by increasing the number of ends to 260. If the exact width is necessary, simply divide the number of remaining threads in half and thread these ends as a twill on both edges of the cloth.

For large patterns, when it's necessary to deal with many remaining ends, straight twill threaded edges may be too regular and repetitive to combine with the pattern selected. Rosepath is more delicate and may work better. Another solution is to choose a section of the pattern that has smaller blocks and use it to fill in to the edges.

Threading and Treadling Conversions

Sometimes an overshot pattern doesn't work out as expected when the weaving is under way. The problem may be that the pattern produced is physically unsuited to the fabric's intended use because the overshot is too long. The resulting floats could catch or sag, quickly ruining the finished cloth. Perhaps the overshot is undesirable because the pattern is just more geometric than the designer intended for that particular project.

Honeycomb

Without changing the threading, both problems can be solved by converting the tie-up and treadling to honeycomb. The resulting cloth has an undulating, textured surface without floats and is particularly suitable for upholstery, bags and lined garments (Figure 67).

The procedure for conversion to honeycomb is simple once the concept of blocks is understood (see Blocks). Patterns in the overshot family of threadings include at least two blocks and many contain four blocks plus tabby. In the more complex four-block, four-harness, overshot drafts, the blocks overlap, producing the speckled or shaded portions of the woven pat-

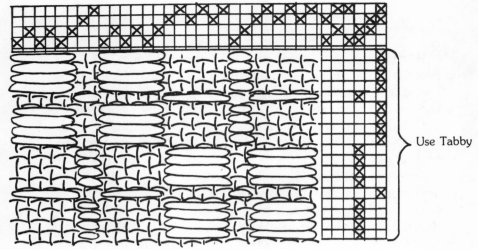

Use Tabby

Overshot Threading and Treadling

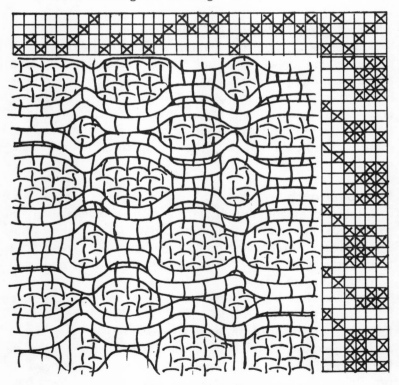

67. Honeycomb from overshot

tern. With honeycomb, the fewer or shorter the overlaps, the crisper the pattern.

The tie-ups and treadlings for these related patterns develop in a fixed manner. Each block is tied to a treadle and that treadle is depressed to create the corresponding overshot. Each overshot is followed by a tabby shot alternating 1–3 and 2–4. A standard four-harness overshot tie-up is used; the treadling sequences are derived directly from each particular overshot threading draft.

To convert an overshot to a honeycomb, the standard overshot tie-up is changed by tying only one harness to each pattern treadle, creating a skeleton tie-up (Figure 22). The tabby treadles tied in the 1–3 and 2–4 combinations remain the same. The treadling for honeycomb is derived from the pattern's original overshot treadling using the simple formula described below.

If the original overshot is:	Honeycomb conversion* is:
Pattern shot 1 (harnesses 1–2) followed by tabby	Treadle 1 using fine thread Treadle 2 using fine thread
Repeat as indicated	Repeat as indicated
	At the end of the block weave 2 shots of tabby (1–3 and 2–4) using coarse or pattern thread
Pattern shot 2 (harnesses 2–3) followed by tabby	Treadle 2 using fine thread Treadle 3 using fine thread
Repeat as indicated	Repeat as indicated
	At the end of the block weave 2 shots of tabby using coarse thread

continued on next page

*This conversion is right side up on a sinking shed loom and wrong side up on a rising shed loom.

If the original overshot is:	Honeycomb conversion* is:
Pattern shot 3 (harnesses 3–4) followed by tabby	Treadle 3 using fine thread Treadle 4 using fine thread
Repeat as indicated	Repeat as indicated
	At the end of the block weave 2 shots of tabby using coarse thread
Pattern shot 4 (harnesses 4–1) followed by tabby	Treadle 4 using fine thread Treadle 1 using fine thread
Repeat as indicated	Repeat as indicated
	At the end of the block weave 2 shots of tabby using coarse thread

Honeycomb derived from overshot may be varied by using only two or three of the four available blocks, using opposite blocks such as 1–2 and 3–4 or 2–3 and 4–1, or by converting only a segment of the original overshot treadling. The curving effect of the tabby lines can be increased or decreased by increasing or decreasing the number of shots in each converted pattern block, respectively. The optical illusion of a coarse lace can be obtained by weaving the pattern blocks with a subdued color and the tabby with a bright or contrasting color.

Inkle Band Weaves

Inkle band weaves, which are drafted in two lines and woven as narrow strips of warp-faced cloth on an inkle loom, can be adapted for wider warp-faced weaves produced on a four-harness loom. These wider warp-faced cloths are useful in combination with the original inkle strips for handsome bags or alone as durable rugs.

To convert the original two-harness draft to a four-harness draft, stack the second pair of one and two threads of the two-harness draft into the three and four harness position in the four-harness draft. This new threading is treadled tabby to produce the same weave as the original inkle draft. The corresponding sett can be determined from the original inkle weaving by measuring the width of the original strip of inkle band and dividing the width into the number of threads in the band. The resulting number is the ends per inch for the four-harness weave.

Inkle weaves can also be converted to a four-harness tapestry with the same design as the original inkle band. In this case, the warp is a plain cotton or linen suitable for tapestry, threaded and treadled as plain weave. The sett is determined by the number of shots per inch in the original inkle weaving. The weft pattern is derived from the original inkle threading draft. Each warp thread of the inkle draft is read as one shot in the tapestry. The number of shots per inch is equal to the number of ends per inch in the inkle weave (Figure 68A and B). The resulting narrow strip of tapestry design might be used as a border or repeated to create a pattern field.

Inkle Draft

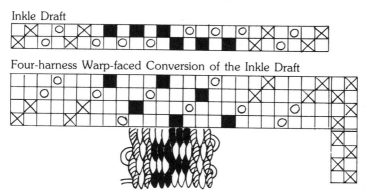

Four-harness Warp-faced Conversion of the Inkle Draft

68A. Inkle draft conversion

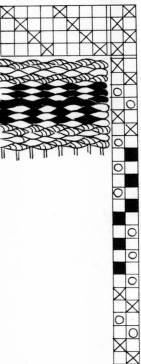

68B. Inkle draft conversion

Card Weaving

Although the warp twist in card weaving is distinctive, as with inkle weaving, card weaving drafts can be converted to four harness, warp-faced weaves. To begin, assign harnesses to the lettered holes of the weaving card as follows:

Hole	Harness
A	1
B	2
C	3
D	4

90

Then, for the up-arrows, thread 1–2–3–4 twill (Figure 69A). When the arrows of the card weaving draft change direction, reverse the twill to 4–3–2–1, omitting the resulting duplication of the point thread. Thus a sample card weaving converts as illustrated in Figure 69.

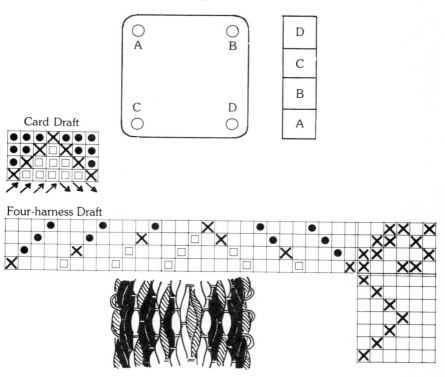

69. A card weaving conversion

Record Sheets

Weaving record sheets increase drafting skills and speed. These printed sheets remind the weaver to record the pertinent information about each piece of weaving and provide a consistent form for enhancing notebooks, sharing weaves with friends and pricing work for sale.

All record sheets should contain several items of basic weaving information:

1. General
    Your name
    The title or description of the weaving
    The date
2. Warp:
    Kind of yarn(s)
       Size/ply
       Color(s)
    Number of threads and length
    Total yardage and weight
    Special arrangements
       Stripes
       Dressings
3. Weft:
    Kind of yarn(s)
       Size/ply
       Color(s)
    Picks per inch
    Yardage and weight
    Special arrangements
4. Loom:
    Width
    Number of harnesses and treadles
    Reed—dents and width
    Sleying
       Ends per dent
       Ends per inch
5. Pattern:
    Complete draft
    Number of repeats
6. Finishing
7. Suggestions and comments

Before creating your own record sheets, consider your specific needs. Are you studying a specific series of weaves? The inclusion of pattern classification, pattern source and pattern name(s) will be of interest to you. The artist interested in creative development might include sketches, graphs and models. The business-oriented weaver records and computes cost by including the hours worked and the hourly rate, the cost of warp and weft and the cost of notions used in finishing.

Computations

While it's true that too much to-do over numbers can spoil the expressive qualities of weaving, it's also true that a piece cut short for lack of warp is, at best, a "happy accident."

Many weavers regularly allow an extra yard for warp lost in the weaving process. This usually works, but a more inclusive calculation of warp length can be worked out to account for a particular loom and the type of cloth produced.

The cloth length is the first and easiest figure to establish. It is simply the desired, finished length to be woven including hems and knots.

The second figure accounts for takeup and shrinkage and is usually estimated at 10% to 20% of the cloth length. However, this percentage approaches zero for tapestry but can increase to 25% and even climb to 50% in fabrics that are warp-faced with extremely lofty wefts. A sample should be woven for questionable weaves and fabrics. By measuring and comparing the warp length, the woven sample just off of the loom and the finished swatch, takeup and shrinkage can be calculated.

Next consider the warp lost to the loom. If a front apron rod is a wooden bar, it takes 3″ just to get around the wood. Thus at least 8″ are necessary to tie-on even with the smallest knots. The number of harnesses and the depth of the castle also influence the warp lost in the process.

Multiharness castles can be a foot deep, as compared to the 2″ allowed the four harnesses on a metal table loom. Allowing 4″ of warp per harness is a good compromise. Although this allows too much waste for a table loom, it accommodates larger looms and it's always better to be on the generous side.

Computing Tapestry Weft

The guesswork can be taken out of computing tapestry weft. By drawing the tapestry on graph paper and weaving a sample to determine the picks per inch, an accurate estimate of the amount of each color can be made.

To convert the graphed drawing of the tapestry to picks, count the number of squares covered by each color in the tapestry. On a second piece of graph paper, rearrange the number of squares for each color in rows the width of the weaving graph. It may be necessary to make rows ½ or ¼ of a square high to stretch a small number of squares across the width of the weaving graph (Figure 70).

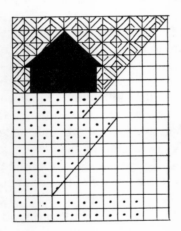
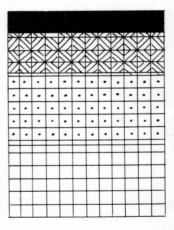

70. Rearrange graph squares

94

Using the tapestry sample, count the actual picks per inch. To find the amount needed of each color, multiply the number of picks per inch by the width in inches of the tapestry plus 25% to allow for takeup. Then multiply this figure by the height in inches of each color stripe derived from the second graph. The resulting figures are the number of inches of each yarn and should be divided by 36 to obtain the number of yards of each color of yarn (Figure 71).

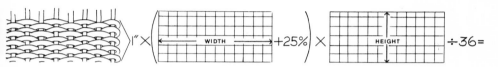

$$1'' \times (\text{WIDTH} + 25\%) \times \text{HEIGHT} \div 36 =$$

71. Computing tapestry weft

Planning Yardage

It is a mistake to try to weave yardage wider than a comfortable arm span, which is usually 32" to 36" wide, and never more than 40". The result of such an attempt will be shabby selvedges and an aching back from leaning to catch the shuttle. It is often faster to weave twice the length of fabric at an easy-to-weave width than to struggle with a too wide piece. To check how wide you can comfortably weave, sit at your loom and extend both arms in the shuttle-catching position without leaning forward. The distance between your hands is your approximate weaving width (Figure 72).

When the intended use of a hand-woven fabric is a garment cut from a purchased pattern, the yardage requirements printed on the pattern can be used in two ways. First, the 36" wide specifications can be followed and the fabric planned to be about 40" in the reed and 10% longer than indicated to allow for shrinkage and possible selvedge defects.

The second method takes a little more planning but works well for jackets with back seams and other garments that do not have pattern pieces placed on the fold. Select the yardage and pattern layout plans for 54″ to 60″ fabrics. Double the length required by the pattern and divide the width in half. Add 10% to both resulting figures to allow for shrinkage. For example, a jacket pattern that calls for 2 yards of 60″ fabric would take 4 ⅖ yards of handwoven fabric 33″ wide. The layout conversion is simple: the hand-woven fabric is folded in half lengthwise rather than from selvedge to selvedge as the layout specifies. Since there are no pieces on the fold, the extra selvedges are not a problem (Figure 73).

72. Arms' reach

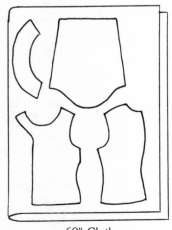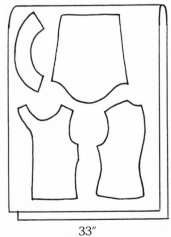

| 60″ Cloth | 33″ |
| Selvedge to Selvedge | Lengthwise |

73. Pattern layout

The Right Size

For those who weave functional items, there are some routine sizes useful in planning proportioned household items and clothing accessories.

Bedspreads are formidable projects but, designed in three panels, they can be woven without much trouble. Each of the three panels should be the length of the bedspread plus an allowance for shrinkage and a hem or finish. The width of the panels may vary according to the width of the bed and the design. For large bedspreads with repetitive patterns, all three panels should be the same size; the width of each panel being one third the total width plus an allowance for shrinkage, seams and hems. In this case, the three panels are sewn together as unobtrusively as possible and then the edges of the spread are either hemmed or fringed. For smaller bedspreads, especially those with a central design, the center panel may be wider than the others—up to the width of the bed. The side panels are then relatively smaller—calculated to complete the width of the spread allowing for shrinkage, seams and hems. A word of warning about a common hand-woven bedspread flaw—they frequently weigh too much. Select materials and weaves that produce a moderate weight cloth. The standard sizes for bedspreads and blankets are:

Bed Size	Bedspread	Blanket
King	120″ × 120″	108″ × 90″
Queen	102″ × 116″	90″ × 90″
Full	96″ × 110″	80″ × 90″
Twin	81″ × 110″	66″ × 90″
Cot	90″ × 90″	60″ × 80″
Crib		36″ × 50″

Place mats are usually about 12″ × 18″, while guest towels, another commonly woven item, are 12″ × 24″.

Clothing accessories are always popular, with $12'' \times 42''$ scarves currently topping the list. Ascots are $8'' \times 36''$. Shawls range from $24'' \times 48''$ to a generous $36'' \times 72''$ for a real warp. Scarves also range in size from $20''$ on a side to a large $36''$ square.

Special Situations

As the weaving horizon broadens, a variety of special situations arise. Each weaver, pursuing a specialized avenue of study, encounters new challenges. Some of these challenges arise from new equipment, such as a double beam, or new materials. The most interesting situations arise from working out new ideas such as eight-harness patterned tubes.

Eight-Harness Patterned Tubes

By graph paper manipulation, a four-harness draft can be converted to an eight-harness draft that produces a tube with four-harness patterns on both sides. Depending on the four harness weave selected, the resulting patterned tube can be used for lacy lanterns, seamless overshot pillows and, woven open at one edge, patterned afghans and bedspreads.

The first step in the process is to recognize that the top layer will be right side up and the bottom layer will be right side down. Thus the draft should take into account this wrap-around concept. To do this, copy the draft of two complete repeats of the selected four-harness draft onto tissue paper. Fold the tissue paper along the repeat line and, without disturbing the position of the folded tissue paper, cut along the fold. Now, slide the bottom piece of tissue paper out from under the upper draft and tape it in position directly above the right-side-up draft (Figure 74).

Proceed to draft the eight harness, patterned, tubular weave by placing the first drafting mark from the right-side-up tissue draft into the appropriate first space of the eight harness draft. The second mark of the eight harness draft is derived from the first mark of the face down part of the tissue draft. The finished eight-harness draft should contain two repeats of the original pattern meshed together.

The treadling and tie-up for this unusual tubular variation are derived in a similar fashion. Draft two repeats of the treadling and tie-up side-by-side on tissue paper, include the tabby for overshots and indicate colors. Fold the tissue along the vertical division between the repeats and cut along the fold. Slide the face down piece of tissue to the right of the face up tissue.

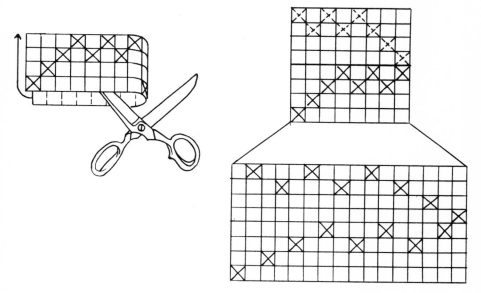

74. Fold, cut and position threading drafts

To complete the tie-up, cut the right-hand tie-up away from its corresponding treadling and slide it up into the "upper four" position of the eight harness tie-up (Figure 75). Draw the new tie-up next to the finished threading draft as follows: the right-side tie-up is drawn exactly as indicated on the tissue; the face-down tie-up actually weaves the face-down, bottom layer of the tube so the weaving, or "up," harnesses must go down and all other harnesses must be tied-up, out of the way of that layer of weaving.

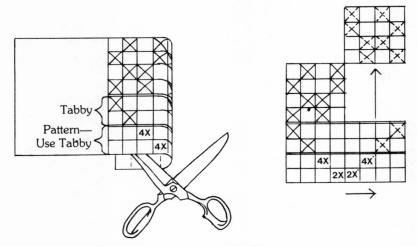

75. Position tie-ups and treadling

The treadling is merged in exactly the same way as the threading. The first mark of the finished treadling is taken from the face-up tissue. The second mark is taken from the face-down tissue. This process is continued until all the treadlings are merged together (Figure 76).

Weaving with an opening at one edge is accomplished by modifying a single shuttle treadling by taking two treadling marks from the left (face-up) tissue and two treadling marks from the right (face-down) treadling. This allows the shuttle to travel to the top edge and back across the upper layer to the center fold, then to the edge of the bottom layer and back to the center fold. Pattern weaves where each pattern shot is followed by tabby shot may also be merged as two shot units so that the tabby follows the pattern shuttle across each layer (Figure 77).

100

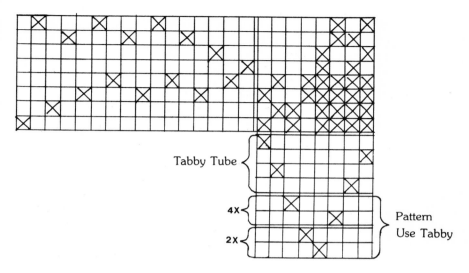

Tabby Tube

4X

2X

Pattern
Use Tabby

76. Finished draft

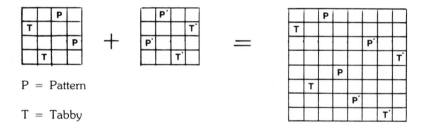

P = Pattern

T = Tabby

77. Merging two shots

Double Beam Tricks

A double beam loom or a supplementary warp device can be used to weave warp yarns of various size and elasticity into a smooth cloth. It is also particularly useful when yarns are similar but the sett varies throughout the piece. Exaggerated lace weaves, where several threads in one dent are followed by one thread in a dent or skipped dents, work out smoothly on a double beam loom. Stuffer warp rugs that gain body from extra unharnessed warp ends which are enclosed in the weaving* and warp patterned cloths where the pattern falls in stripes between plain areas are also best woven on a double beam loom (Figure 78). Even weaves such as M's and O's, where the warp threads collapse into groups predominantly in one area, benefit from a double beam.

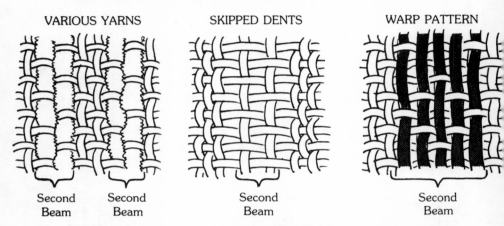

78. **Various yarns, skipped dents or patterns**

A double-beam loom can also be used to produce intentional ripples, puckers and loose threads for special design effects such as seersucker and terry cloth. A double-beam is necessary to produce a variety of double weaves including those with unequal length layers, or layers of equal length but each with a different sett, or those with a different size of yarn in each layer.

Weaving a single layer, double beam piece can be tricky. In the case of two warps that produce one unpuckered cloth, or even one intentionally rippled surface, the two tensions must be checked frequently by releasing the loom brakes and ex-

---

* Stuffer warps work best on counterbalance or counter march looms where a shed is created by both the rising and sinking of harnessed warp, thus allowing the weaving to envelop the stuffer warp.

amining the cloth for proper surface development. This is especially necessary when the two warps are made of yarns having differing elasticity. Under tension the more elastic yarns may seem to be equally taut but, when the tension is released, the elastic yarns will contract and pucker the cloth. Thus, in this situation, it is usually necessary to weave with the more elastic warp looser than the warp with more stable yarns. A similar situation is encountered with warps of thick and thin yarns and warps with varying setts. In these cases the two tensions start out the same but the closer sett or thick warp yarn becomes tighter as the weaving progresses because more of these yarns are taken-up in the weaving process (Figure 78). To weave a smooth cloth, periodically release the close sett or thick warp yarn without advancing the finer or widely spaced warp.

Weaving double layer fabric structures is actually a little easier to control. Several methods seem to work equally well. The simplest approach is to weave several shots (up to several inches) on the bottom warp, release the warp tension on that layer and weave the same distance on the upper warp. When weaving two layers with a different sett or different sized yarns in each layer, add extra shots to the layer with the open sett or fine yarns and release the tension more frequently in the layer with the close sett or thick yarns so that the weaving of both layers progresses at the same rate (Figure 79).

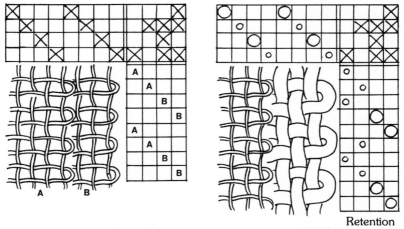

Retention

79. Weave extra shots on open-sett layer

Planning the warp lengths for such double-beam projects needs special consideration. Warps of heavier, stretchier or closely sett yarns must be longer than the corresponding warps of finer, more stable, or wider spaced yarns. The difference can be anywhere from 10% to a whopping 50%. Although these percentage figures can be estimated, with a little extra allowed for error in the longer warp, the best approach is to weave samples from equal-length warps of the various materials and setts. Samples of equal length under tension should be removed from the loom, finished as the intended cloth will be finished and then carefully measured for shrinkage. The warp thrums remaining on the loom should also be compared for amounts lost in takeup.

The total difference in fabric shrinkage and warp takeup can be used to calculate the necessary difference in warp lengths. In the following example there are two 10″ samples from 40″ warps:

	Sample 1 (Stable or Finer Yarns)	Sample 2 (Stretchy or Heavy Yarn)
Tie-on	10″	10″
Woven Length Under Tension	10″	10″
Finished Cloth	9″	8″
Warp Remaining	19″	17″
Loss	40″ − 38″ = 2″ for every 10″	40″ − 35″ = 5″ for every 10″
Percentage	2/10 = 20%	5/10 = 50%

For this project, the second warp would have to be 30% (50% − 20%) longer than the first warp.

Chapter 4:

Dressing the Loom

Warp Winding

Winding a warp correctly contributes to the weaving process. Weavers who wind sloppy warps pay for their carelessness with dropped crosses, tangles and broken ends.

Once the warp length has been determined, it is easy to arrange the necessary parts of the warping board or reel by using a guide string. Cut one string the length of the total warp plus 8″ to allow for a knot at each end. Tie one end of this guide string to the outer peg of the cross on the top member of the warping board or reel. Work the string around the reel or board until the end of the string is at a point where it can be tied to a peg. If necessary, move a peg to the closest possible position to the string end. This method saves figuring how far apart the pegs of a board are or how many yards in a turn on the mill (Figure 80).

The first consideration in winding a consistent warp is reeling the warp yarns smoothly off balls, spools or cones. It is almost impossible to wind a good warp off skeins. The rhythm and even tension necessary to wind a warp can never be established when the swift or skein winder constantly interrupts with minor catches or loops of thread. Even cones and spools can sometimes present similar problems. When these problems arise, wind the contrary material off onto a ball winder or into carefully wound bobbins, then proceed.

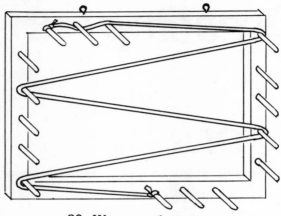

80. Warp guide string

A counting thread can save plenty of frustration and time by separating the warp being wound into manageable groups. These groups usually contain about ten threads. The size of the group is not as important as the convenience of not having to count all the threads individually. The number of threads in a group can be related to the number of ends in the warp or to pattern repeats. The process is easy. Cut a 24″ length of string and loop it around the warping board or reel frame between the pegs that form the cross. Wind the predetermined number of ends in a group. Bring the upper end of the string over the warped group. Bring the lower end of the string around from under the group and toss it over the group into the upper position (Figure 81). Proceed to wind the next group of warp ends and repeat the string process.

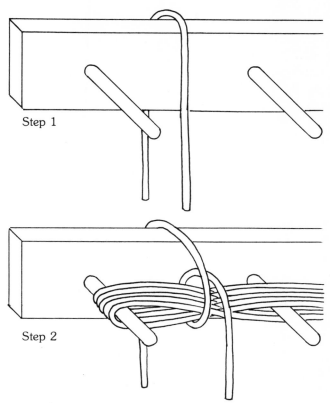

Step 1

Step 2

81. Marking a warp group

When a wound warp is still on the warping board or mill, rather than tying the cross with string, try using mini lease sticks. Made of a ½" diameter dowel that has been cut into 5" lengths, sanded and drilled on the ends to accommodate waxed shoe lace ties, these mini lease sticks make it easier to find the cross when the warp is taken off the mill and again when the warp is finally put on the loom (Figure 82).

Large warps are easier to deal with when wound in sections, rather than one large mass. Chain off finished sections and mark them as to position on the lease sticks. Leave the guide string on the warping reel to assure identical warp section lengths.

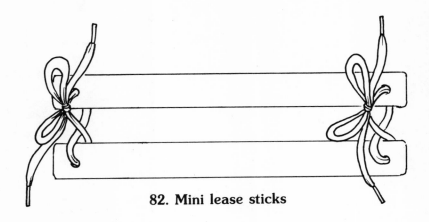

82. Mini lease sticks

Additional Ends

Did you ever run out of warp material before the desired number of ends was wound? If you have compatible material, all is not lost. Of course, the other material can be wound as just a continuation of the original warp. A better solution, however, is to replan the warp, interspersing the additional ends as stripes of any size from two ends to a band down the center of the warp.

First, count the number of warp ends wound. Tie the cross and chain off this original piece of warp. Subtract the number of ends warped from the total ends planned and wind a second warp to make up the rest of the ends.

Put a set of lease sticks in both warps sections and tie the two sets of sticks to the loom. Spread both warp sections in the raddle according to a predetermined stripe pattern.

A third set of lease sticks merge the two warps into one cross. Working according to the example in Figure 83, pick up the first group of warp threads from stick one. Pick up the next stripe from stick three and proceed to pick up all threads passing over lease sticks one and three in the planned stripe order. Secure the pickup lease stick five and remove sticks one and three, being careful to retain the position of the threads on sticks two and four. Using the same procedure, merge the threads passing over lease sticks two and four onto stick six. Secure lease stick six to lease stick five and remove sticks two and four. This completes the merging of the two warp sections.

108

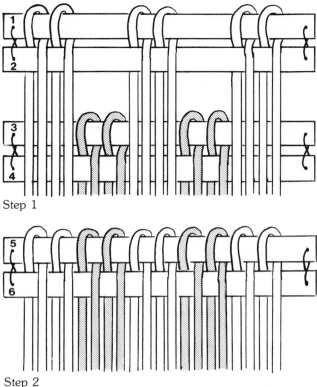

Step 1

Step 2

83. Merging two sets of lease sticks

Beaming

Although there's more than one way to dress a loom, the process commonly misnomered back-to-front* allows for the beaming of very delicate materials, since the warp only travels through the heddles and reed one way. With this method, it's also easier to beam a warp evenly because the loop ends of the warp are not cut and retied thereby unavoidably varying the length of the warp threads.

* Back-to-front and front-to-back originally referred to whether the harness nearest the weaver was first in the threading order (front-to-back) or whether farthest from the weaver was considered first (back-to-front) because the threads encounter it first.

Either a raddle made of 1" × 1" lumber with common nails spaced at 1" intervals or a coarse reed can be used to spread the warp to the weaving width. Rubber bands stretched around the nail heads can be used to secure the warp groups in the raddle. Plastic-tipped shoe strings are ideal for holding lease sticks together. They are easy to thread through the sticks and seldom break or fray.

Before the warp is beamed, any warp ends that are not in the cross may be positioned by tying them to the lease stick they should have gone under (Figure 84).

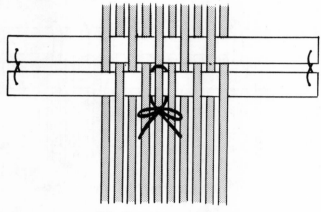

84. Cross correction

Beaming a large warp is best performed by two people. The person tensioning the warp should hold it firmly rather than letting it slide through their fingers. Instead of combing or brushing the warp repeatedly, remove tangles by shaking or lightly striking the warp.

Computer listing paper is an ideal material for separating the layers of warp on the back beam. A roll of heavy craft paper is more substantial for wide, heavily tensioned warps. Without resorting to sticks, the sturdiest material for this beaming job is single-sided corrugated paper available as window dresser's backdrop from display companies.

Threading the Heddles

That dreaded chore, threading the heddles, has to be done so, at least, it should be as easy as possible. Get comfortable. If the breast of the loom folds or lifts off, get in close to the harness with a low chair. Bring the lease sticks forward, within easy reach. If necessary, prop up the harnesses so you don't have to stoop to work.

Next, count the heddles on each harness and add extras as needed for a particular warp and threading. Place the correct number of heddles in each area of the harness frames. This is very important if the loom has clips on the bottom of the harness frames that become inaccessible when the heddles are threaded.

To reduce eye strain from looking at each warp end, work with groups of four ends at a time. Locate and position the first four heddles to be threaded. Pick up the first four ends, placing them in order over the index finger, the middle finger and the ring and little fingers of the left hand. Thread these four ends, check them for errors and proceed to the next group of four (Figure 85).

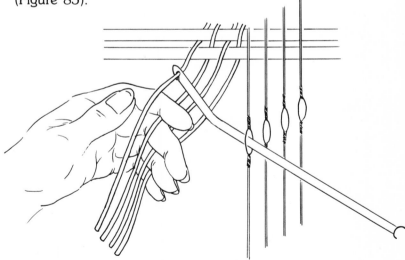

85. Threading a group of 4 warp ends

Color coding the harnesses seems to help weavers threading multiharness or narrow castle looms. Painting the lower heddle bar of each harness frame a different color helps to visually separate the shafts. String heddles can be dyed a different color for each harness (avoid dark or close shades).

For those who don't like to use a long reed hook but wish their finger nails were longer and stronger to separate and pick up threads, a thimble hook can be made by soldering a piece of wire to the side of a thimble so that it extends beyond the end of the thimble to form a hook. A similar hook can be cut out of silver and bent to fit the index finger (Figure 86).

Tie threaded pattern repeats or several groups of four into loose, overhand loop knots. This easily removed knot prevents accidental unthreading and prepares the warp for sleying.

86. Finger hooks

Sleying the Reed

Again, as with threading, get comfortable. Place the reed flat and in front of the harnesses, using extra lease sticks laid across the loom to manage the reed's position. Mark the center of the reed and the center of the beater with strings for reference (Figure 87). These strings can be left indefinitely on the whole reed collection. Ideally, use a flat, double-ended reed hook to draw the threads down through the reed. If a heddle hook must do double duty, turn it over and use it more like a knife than a hook, bringing the warp through the reed with a curving action (Figure 88).

112

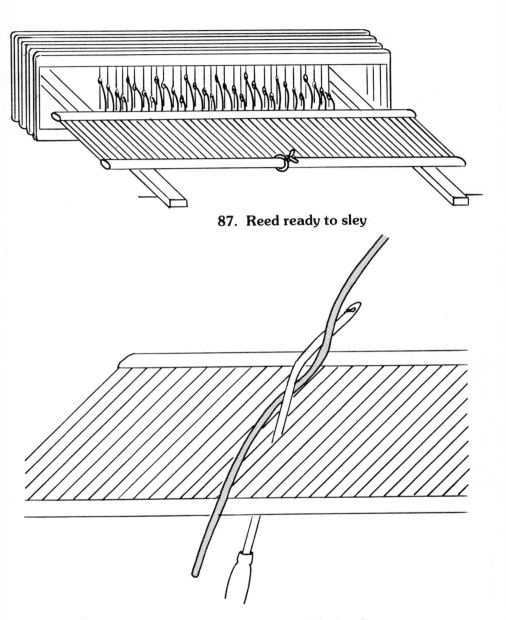

87. Reed ready to sley

88. Sleying with a heddle hook

To feed the warp ends to the reed hook in order, treadle a tabby while holding an unknotted section of warp with the left hand. Insert your left middle finger in the shed created in the group. Treadle the other tabby and insert your left index finger in this second shed. Pick off each end in turn with the reed hook as it is passed through the reed (Figure 89).

Secure the warps in the reed and mount the reed in the beater.

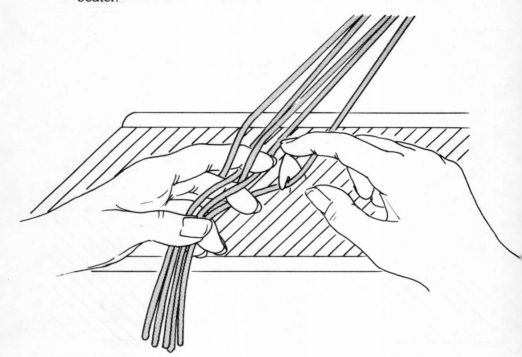

89. Speed sleying

Tying-on

Although there are some ingenious ways to attach the warp to the apron, there are no secrets to successfully tying-on an even-tensioned warp; it's all work and patience. A few proce-

114

dures do make the job move faster. Use a second apron rod (see Loom Maintenance) instead of tying the knots in the slots of the apron.

Although many small knots consume time, fewer, larger knots are unwieldy and increase the weaving necessary to spread the warp. Knots can vary from four ends to 2″ using personal preference as a guide.

Begin tying on by attaching a group of ends from each edge to the apron rod. Passing the threads around the rod, split the group in half and tie an adjustable half knot. The next knotted group is placed halfway between the first knots. The next two knots halve the new spaces created by the middle knot. This dividing process eliminates many side to side tensioning problems because the pull is always evenly distributed.

When all the threads are tensioned, the half knots may be secured with half bows. However, square knots can also be used since the correctly tied knot is easily released (Figure 90).

Step 1   Step 2

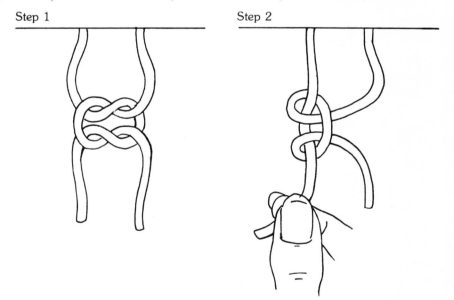

90. Square knot release

Threading Corrections

Now the moment of truth arrives. The first tabby sheds will reveal most threading mistakes. Two threads twisted between the harnesses and the reed will not open. When two threads are twisted between the harnesses, usually only one will shed. These are easy to spot and, though time consuming, easy to repair. The same is true for skipped spaces in the reed.

More difficult problems involve the omission, transposition or repetition of part of a threading pattern. If the error is an isolated transposition, merely rethread the problem section. One repeated thread can be discarded over the back of the loom and the reed resleyed leaving the empty heddle in place.

When the correction involves moving an end to another harness or threading new ends, repair heddles will be needed. These extra heddles can be added in a variety of ways to accommodate one or more missed threads. A string heddle can be added whether your loom has string, wire or flat heddles. To make a string heddle, cut a piece of smooth, strong, fine string twice the total length of a heddle plus 6". Place the string under the lower heddle bar and pull the ends of the string together, tying overhand knots to match the top and bottom of the existing heddle eyes. To finish the heddle, tie the ends of the string snugly to the upper heddle bar.

A quicker fix for flat steel or wire heddles involves sacrificing an unused heddle. Bend the ends of the heddle back to form flat V's. Tie the heddle in place with strings passed under the V's and over the heddle bars.

Flat heddles can be jury-rigged by opening the ends of an unused heddle with wire cutters. Snip one side of each heddle end near the base of the heddle bar opening. Spring the repair heddle in place by bending the cut ends around the heddle bar. Be sure to remove these weakened heddles when the piece is finished.

By lighting a wooden match under a wire heddle, the solder holding the wire twist can be softened and removed with a sharp tap. The heddle can then be untwisted and placed in the repair position.

On a string heddle loom, heddles can be moved from the end of a heddle bar to any repair location. Simply untie the knotted end of the selected repair heddle and pass the heddle through the existing threaded heddles. When the repair heddle is in position, retie the loose heddle ends to the heddle bar (Figure 91).

New warp ends may be necessary to correct a threading. These extra ends can be wound on a bobbin or spool and either weighted or tied to produce a tension equivalent to the rest of the warp.

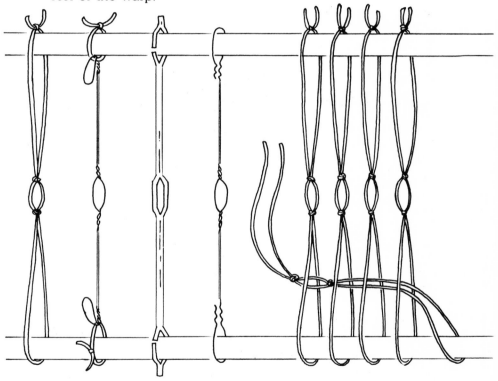

91. Repair heddles

Chapter 5:

Weaving Secrets

Weaving Finesse

The weaving process abounds with tricks and secrets, most the result of years of experience. Every facet of the process can be smoothed and improved with practice.

Treadling

Rearranging the treadle tie-ups can increase weaving speed and help to keep track of which shot is next as well. For single shuttle weaves, try treadle "dancing." From right to left, the treadles are depressed in the following order:

Treadle	Foot
1	right
3	left
2	right
4	left

By retying the harnesses to fit this pattern, both feet can be used without confusion (Figure 92).

When weaving patterns with a tabby, coordinate the tabby treadles with the tabby shuttle so that the right tabby treadle is depressed when the tabby shuttle is entering from the right. The tabby shuttle entering from the left would, of course, indicate the left tabby treadle should be depressed. The pattern treadles may be placed either to the right or left of the tabby treadles or even in between them. Whatever arrangement is used should be adhered to so that treadling becomes almost automatic.

Standard Tie-up   "Dancing" Tie-up

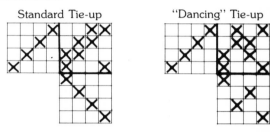

92. Treadle dancing twill conversion

Beating

Beating seems a cut and dried subject, yet an experienced weaver knows that the timing, position and force of the beater all influence the web produced.

The timing of the beater swing can help to clear the shed. At the end of a beat, push the batten back over the shed as the next treadle is being depressed, thus combing the open shed. For firm fabrics beat a second time before the next shot is made. After the shot, the beater is pulled as the shed is lowered.

The beater position either adds or subtracts from the force of the beat. For delicate warps requiring a gentle beat, advance the warp frequently, never letting the web advance more than 3" or 4" in front of the beater. This process also reduces wear from the friction of the beater.

119

Open lace weaves require expert beater control and a tight warp. The rhythm that develops during the five-shot pattern units is an interesting "pull gently, pull gently, beat, beat, beat."

On the other hand, rugs should have the firmest beat provided by a full swing of the beater. Drive home each shot with one big swing rather than lots of little whacks. Extra weight can be added to a lightweight beater to increase the beating force.

Handling Shuttles

Good shuttles are made of hardwood and are fastidiously smooth, especially the bottoms of boat shuttles. Boat shuttles are used when speed and rhythm are important. They are thrown across the shed along the shuttle race with the yarn opening facing the weaver. For wide warps and heavy yarns, use large shuttles with weighted ends for better travel.

Flat shuttles are ideal for smaller warps. To work smoothly, the shuttles should be about the same width as the warp. If the shuttle is too short, the weaver must reach into the shed to retrieve it. If the shuttle is too long, it is hard to remove from the shed.

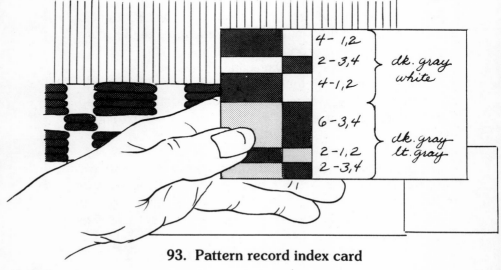

93. Pattern record index card

Two colors can be wound on one flat shuttle by winding each color, figure eight style, on a side of the shuttle. This technique also applies to a situation where a very long, continuous weft is desired on a flat shuttle. Both sides can be wrapped and then the center can be filled.

Keeping Track

Those who enjoy pattern weaves have methods of keeping track of where they are in a particular piece. The most common way is to tape the treadling instructions to the castle of the loom. If a loom doesn't have a castle, the top of the first harness will do. Instead of taping up a pattern repeat that is less than 5″ long, record the first pattern repeat full size on a 3″ × 5″ card. Include all the weaving information and use the card as a guide for future repeats of the pattern (Figure 93).

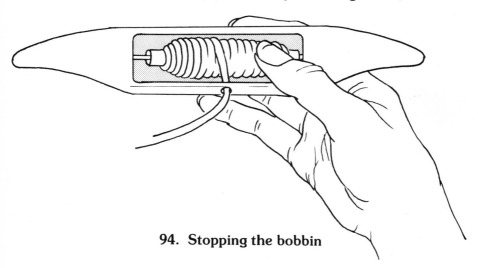

94. Stopping the bobbin

To make two pieces of weaving the exact same length, begin by recording the exact length of the first piece under tension. A strip of ribbon or a cloth tape measure pinned to the beginning of the first piece and carried along with the weaving can act as an accurate measure. Use the same process to make the second piece exactly the same length.

121

Selvedges

Selvedges and weft takeup can be controlled by proper shuttle catching. Stop the shuttle from discharging yarn at the end of a shot by dropping the shuttle catching hand after a shot. For more tension, stop the bobbin with the thumb as the shuttle is caught (Figure 94). For really bouncy wefts, fasten a small piece of fuzzy yarn inside the shuttle and thread it out through the yarn opening to slow the discharge of the weft.

The weft should be placed correctly at the selvedge edge and should describe approximately a 15° angle across the warp. Each weft thread may be put in place at the selvedge with the fingers of the shuttle-throwing hand, but this practice is time-consuming and breaks the rhythm of the weaving process. Although there are some warps that seem to need special selvedge attention because their warps pull in and break, even this problem can sometimes be alleviated. Put a little more tension on the warp, work slowly and switch to a lightweight shuttle with a large yarn opening to cut down the shuttle momentum and drag which pulls in edges and, in turn, causes them to bind in the reed and finally break.

Good selvedges are related to properly wound bobbins. When the weaving is interrupted by tangles and catches in the weft thread as it comes off the bobbin, the selvedge may show unevenness (see Bobbins).

One common selvedge flaw is a characteristic ridge or ripple effect caused by a combination of too much weft incorporated in the shot ending at that side of the cloth and too little weft incorporated in the following shot. This can be attributed to the difference between how the left and right hands throw and catch the shuttle, but, more likely, it is produced by changing the shed before the weft is beaten into place. With each shot the problem becomes worse as the shed changes and weft tensions interact (Figure 95). The cure is to gently pull the weft shot ending at the offending selvedge after the shot has been beaten and before the next shed is treadled. After four shots in this manner, the problem should be corrected and the weaving can progress in a normal manner, taking care to beat each shot before the next shed is opened.

Some weaves yield inherently bad selvedges because of floats or, as in the case of twill, a non-woven edge thread caused by the interaction of the threading, treadling and shuttle direction. In twill weaves where an end is left out at both selvedges, the solution is to change the direction of the shuttle to incorporate the ends. Thus, if the shuttle went from left to right, discontinue the weft at the end of that shot, depress the next treadle in the sequence and again throw the shuttle from left to right. This change should pick up both warp ends by the end of a treadling sequence.

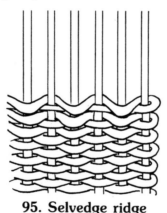

95. Selvedge ridge

When an end is dropped from one selvedge of a twilled cloth, changing the direction of the shuttle will only move the end to the other selvedge. There are several solutions, not the least of which is discarding one end. A better solution in this and other selvedge situations is to wind two shuttles with the same weft and alternate these shuttles throughout a weave which would otherwise require only one shuttle. The twining of the weft threads, which happens naturally with the methodical alternation of shuttles, will produce a neat selvedge no matter which threading is used.

123

Threading four ends of twill at each edge is sufficient to improve the selvedges of overshot weaves (see Justifying).

When a very solid edge is desired on a patterned piece such as a rug, one thread on each edge can be left unharnessed. Then, as the weaving progresses, the weft can be passed around the edge thread by hand.

A firm decorative edge for rugs results from threading a weaving card with yarns which compliment the weave at each selvedge. All four ends of each card are threaded in one dent and weighted or tied to the back of the loom. The cards are positioned just in front of the harnesses and turned each time the shed is changed—or every second or third time as needed to balance the weaves. This selvedge treatment blends beautifully with beginning and ending rows or weft twining (Figure 96).

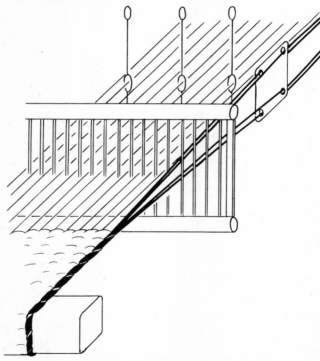

96. Card woven selvedges

Broken Warp

Every weaver hates it and yet it happens in the best of warps. Occasionally a warp thread breaks and must be repaired.

Warp Repair

The usual way to repair a warp is to thread in a repair end, pin it to the cloth and tension it by tying it to the broken end at the back of the loom. When the cloth is off the loom, the pin holding the repair is removed and the resulting ends are needle-woven into the cloth.

If the warp and the weft are the same, and especially if they are slubby, the following warp repair is quick and almost invisible. Using a bow knot, tie a length of warp repair thread to the broken end at the back beam. Bring the repair thread through the appropriate heddle and reed slot. Then, rather than pinning or tying the repair thread to the broken end at the cloth, simply pass the broken thread around the repair thread and into the shed with the weft. Tuck the repair thread in the same shed but in the opposite direction from the mend. Weave two shots and adjust the tension on the mended thread by simultaneously pulling gently on the ends tucked into the shed (Figure 97).

97. Warp repair

Prevention

Of course, warp breakage can be avoided by employing only the smoothest and strongest materials. But what about the range of interesting materials that fall into the warping "gray area"? By observing some special weaving practices, most breaks can be avoided.

For yarns that fray, go fuzzy and finally break, avoid any kind of friction. Warp the loom using a raddle and handle the warp as little as possible. Start each shed one harness at a time with the beater at the fell. Move the beater gingerly over as short a distance as possible and avoid repetitive beats.

Sudden treadling can cause delicate, fine yarns to snap. Too deep a shed also puts undue stress on a fine warp. To decrease the shed, either treadle lightly or retie the treadles, allowing for less travel. Beater velocity increases the probability of breakage as does allowing the lease sticks to creep up close to the heddles.

Warps that are extremely sensitive to tension changes caused by treadling and beating can be warp weighted. By releasing the loom tension and adding a tensioning beam, the conversion can be made without rewarping. Install a 1″ × 1″ (or 2″ × 4″ for large warps) piece of lumber the length of the warp beam between the warp threads and the beam. Hang enough weight from the ends of the lumber to establish the tension necessary to weave (Figure 98).

Saving Graces

Whether a weaving problem is inherent in the weave, the result of miscalculation or poor design, certain tricks make the difference between real trouble and successful weaving.

Double weave is an example of a weave with inherent problems. Although it is perfect on the side facing the weaver, the hidden side is troublesome. A hand mirror can be used to look at the underside of the work, but this is a slow process and mistakes can't be spotted as they happen. The weaver has to put down the shuttle, pick up the mirror and lean over the

126

progressing weaving. However, for a few dollars and a trip to the automotive supplies store, the loom can sport a car rear-view mirror. This mirror can be mounted with screws to a front upright or side horizontal support of the loom. The mirror is aimed so that the weaver can glance in it to see the underside of the weaving as it progresses. To figure out where to mount the mirror, get a friend to hold it in various positions while the weaver sits in a comfortable weaving position and looks in the mirror (Figure 99).

Twills are commonly sleyed with too few ends per inch, usually because the weaver forgets that a sett suitable for plain weave is not close enough for twill. In such a case, tabby can be treadled alone or the twill can be treadled as a pattern with tabby between each pattern shot. If all else fails, resley the warp in a denser reed, wind it forward and respace it on the back beam. After the warp is wound back onto the warp beam, retie the warp to the apron and begin anew.

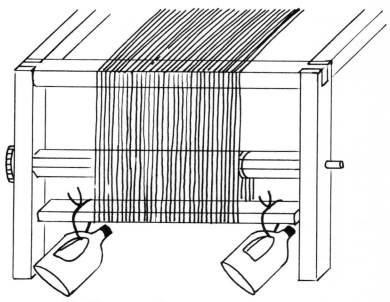

98. Warp weighting to prevent breakage

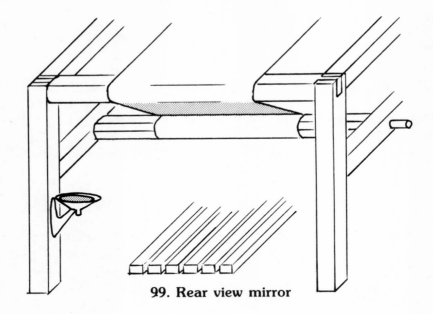

99. Rear view mirror

Perhaps the most discouraging problem is a design with something missing. The weaver's bag of tricks should include some basic accent ideas to spark waning weavings.

Tapestries, rugs, wall hangings and heavy but decorative garments benefit from pile techniques such as soumak, twining, pulled loops and rya knots (Figure 100). Bumpy knots tied in the weft before it is wound on the shuttle can create an interesting texture on an otherwise nondescript surface. Even pieces of yarn simply laid-in along with the weft sparkle on a drab surface. For a more obviously designed inlay, try a variation of Swedish dukagång. Working right side down on a warp threaded twill, treadle three harnesses up and lay in the pattern thread according to a geometric or regular design. Weave a shot of tabby and again treadle the same three harnesses up for a pattern inlay (Figure 101). The resulting pattern areas have regular vertical lines and are best suited to highly structured or geometric designs originally composed on graph paper.

128

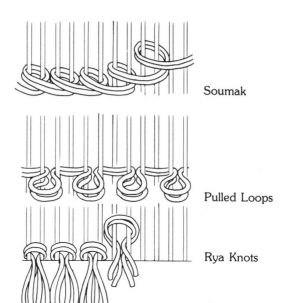

Soumak

Pulled Loops

Rya Knots

100. Pile techniques

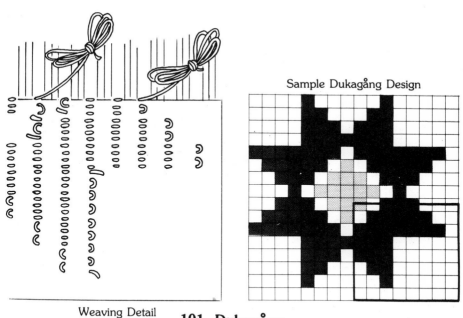

Sample Dukagång Design

Weaving Detail

101. Dukagång

Fine or lacy fabrics can also be accented with inlay, which is especially attractive in translucent/opaque design arrangements, as well as with leno twists and Danish medallion (Figure 102).

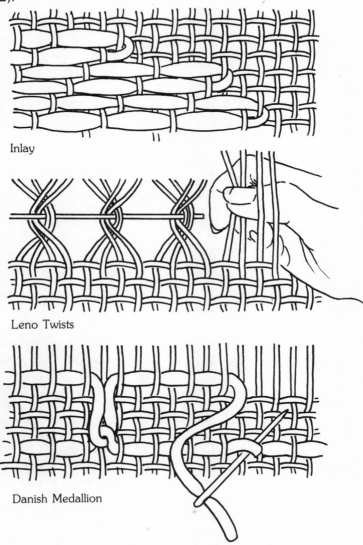

Inlay

Leno Twists

Danish Medallion

102. Lace techniques

A simple one shuttle, two-color technique can convert a monotonous twill into a striking two-color weft pattern without sacrificing weaving speed to the handling of two shuttles. One color is wound on the shuttle in the usual manner. A cone or pull-string ball of the second color is placed on the floor to the left side of the loom and near the shed. The shuttle is thrown from the right to the left and a loop of yarn from the cone is picked up and pulled back into the same shed by the weft as the shuttle is sent back from the left to the right. How far the loop is pulled back into the shed determines the design. The same process is repeated for every treadle change (Figure 103).

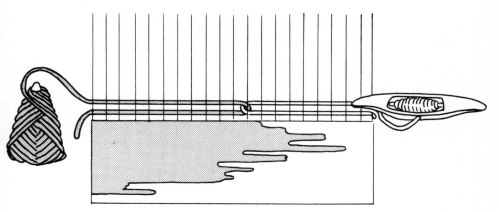

103. Two-color weft pattern

Taking this idea one step further, three colors can be worked in the same manner by placing a third color ball or cone in position on the right side of the loom. Following the same procedure, when the shuttle is returned left to right, pick up a loop from the third color yarn and throw the shuttle right to left, beginning the process again (Figure 104).

This technique may require some adjustments in the weaving plans since there is a double thickness of weft yarn in each shed. Weaving an unbalanced 3–1 twill accentuates the weft pattern. The direction of the twill can also be changed to echo directional changes of the pattern. Although the patterns created by this technique are not hard edged, shadows and shading can be developed by establishing two design lines that define a central area and pulling the cone weft alternately first to the left line in the first shed and then to the right line in the following shed (Figure 105). The variations on this idea increase for the three color technique as two more lines are introduced for the third color to follow.

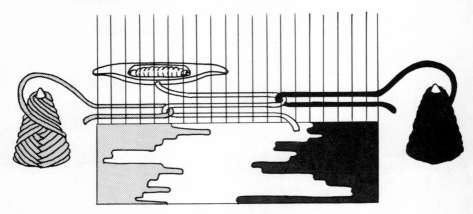

104. Three-color weft pattern

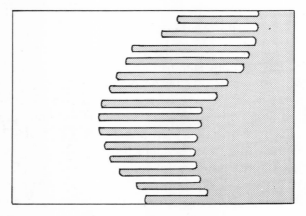

105. Two-color shading

Needlework incorporated into weaving rescues a dull piece without destroying the woven surface. Any type of needlework can be applied to weaving with good results as long as the technique and materials are carefully selected to work with weaving. Running stitch, back stitch, chain stitch and blanket stitch all add texture and pattern to waning designs. Couching stitches can be used to stitch down ridges of material (Figure 106).

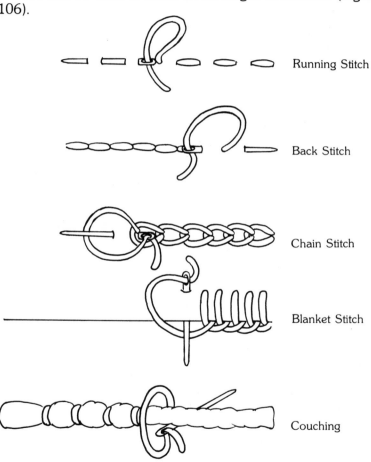

Running Stitch

Back Stitch

Chain Stitch

Blanket Stitch

Couching

106. Needlework stitches

133

Many fabrics lend themselves to counted-thread embroidery. Canvas weaves and monk's cloth readily accept cross stitch and its relatives. Huck weaves claim their own embroidery technique of the same name based on the cloth's regular arrangement of floating warp threads. Wide, geometric borders of huck embroidery look deceptively complex but actually work progresses quickly. Huck embroidery is worked as rows of running stitches through the warp floats, interrupted by shifts from one row to another. The choice of close shades of shiny floss or needlework wool produces pattern areas rather than separate dotted lines of color (Figure 107).

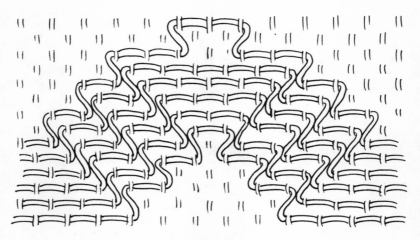

107. Huck embroidery

Chapter 6:

Almost Finished

Finishing begins before the warp goes on the loom. In the planning stages decisions are made about the final form of a piece. Will a garment be shaped on the loom? Will there be slits for buttonholes and pockets? Will a tapestry have a hem or will the edge be twined and braided? These and other decisions need to be made in the design process.

Finishes on the Loom

Finishing begins on the loom. For example, weft twining is a weaving technique that is also used to begin and end a tapestry or rug because it spaces the warp and doesn't ravel, thus creating a solid weft edge for the warp finish. Using two butterflies and working either right to left or left to right, begin by passing butterfly A under the first warp thread. Pass butterfly B under the second warp thread and continue across the warp by alternately passing butterflies A and B under the succeeding warp threads (Figure 108).

108. Weft twining

Hemstitch, the daintiest finish for linens, should be worked on the loom where the tension acts as a perfectly taut embroidery frame. Since the finished stitches hold the weft in place there is no need for filler between separate pieces of cloth on the same warp. Embroidery books describe variations on this stitch, but the best one for hand weaving gains its durability from piercing the cross of warp and weft threads directly below a group of warp threads caught in the stitch's looped knot.

Working right to left, the stitch begins by bringing a threaded, sharp needle from the right to the left behind the first group of three (or five) warp ends. Allow the slack sewing thread to form a loop on the cloth. The needle then travels to the right, behind the same group of warp ends. From the back, the point of the needle pierces the center warp and weft cross two or three picks down the cloth. The needle continues up through the cloth and the thread loop, pulling the slack out of the thread loop and tying a knot around the group of warp threads (Figure 109A and B).

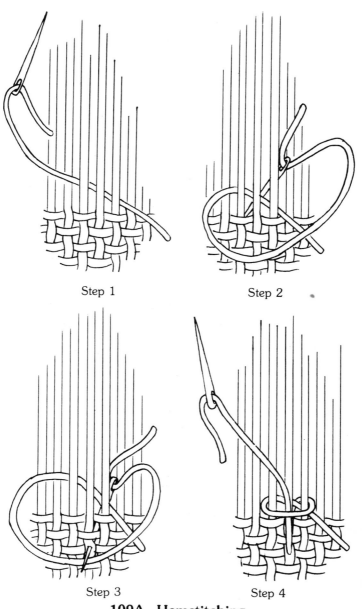

Step 1

Step 2

Step 3

Step 4

109A. Hemstitching

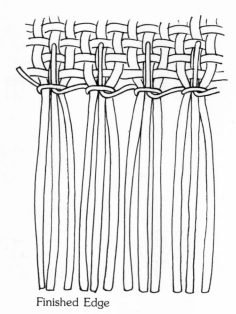

Finished Edge

109B. Hemstitching

Some of the nicest buttonholes for hand woven garments are those designed right along with the garment. The slit woven buttonhole enhances heavy woven garments where a needle worked buttonhole would be impossible. Simply plan the placement and size of the buttonholes and transfer the buttonhole marks to the warp on the loom. Weave a tapestry slit using two butterflies wherever a buttonhole is indicated (Figure 110).

Cord button loops can be worked at or near the selvedge edge as the weaving progresses. Begin each loop by throwing a shot of cord toward the edge where the loop is desired. Weave from ¼" to 1½" using regular weft. Weave the next shot of button cord leaving a loop at the selvedge edge.

To form a self facing for a garment or to hide unavoidably irregular selvedges, carry the cord shot to within 1" of the selvedge and bring it out of the shed to form the loop on the surface of the weaving. Weave the regular weft as needed and return the cord to the weaving 1" from the selvedge. When the weaving is finished, the 1" extension can be folded back to form a self facing (Figure 111).

Decorative button loops are developed by weaving two shots of cord, half hitching the first cord around the second cord at the selvedge edge to form a knotted loop. Finish the button loop by weaving the second cord and then the first cord back into the cloth.

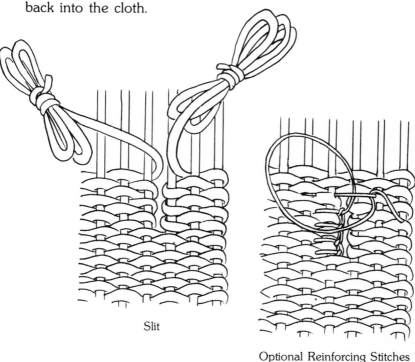

Slit

Optional Reinforcing Stitches

110. Buttonhole slit

A variety of buttons can be incorporated into woven garments in the same manner as the cord button loops. The button, bead or button knot is placed on the cord allowing for one generous shot length on either side of the button position.

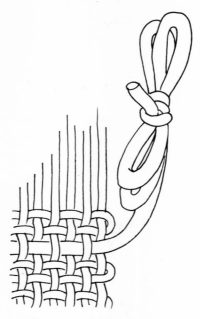

Beginning Button Loop

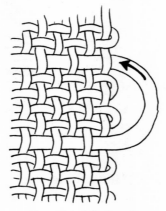

Completed Button Loop

111. Button loop and variations

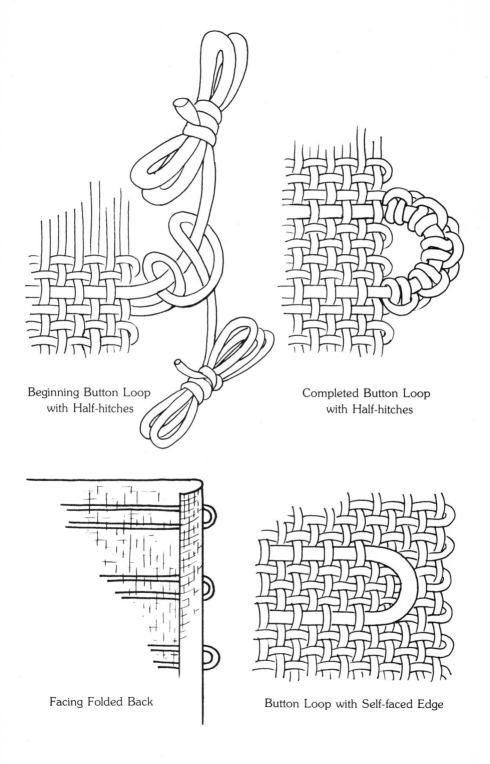

Beginning Button Loop
with Half-hitches

Completed Button Loop
with Half-hitches

Facing Folded Back

Button Loop with Self-faced Edge

Weave one shot length into the cloth, positioning the button, bead, or button knot either at the edge or 1″ from the edge for a self facing. The cord can be woven back immediately; or as in the button loop procedures, weave from ¼″ to 1½″ of regular weft and then weave in the other end of the button cord (Figure 112).

A variation of the slit buttonhole and woven loop produces an intricate closure using only one button. Weave a series of ½″ to 1″ slits along the buttonhole edge of the fabric, spacing them 1″ apart. On the button side of the garment weave 1½″ to 2″ loops to match the buttonholes. Sew a button approximately 1″ above the last slit.

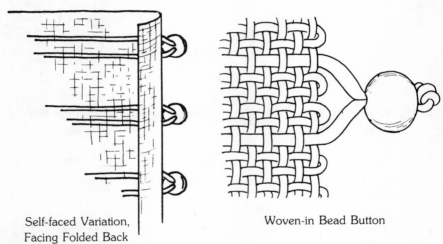

Self-faced Variation,
Facing Folded Back

Woven-in Bead Button

112. Woven-in button

To fasten the garment, thread the loops through the corresponding buttonholes. Starting at the bottom, pull the second loop through the first loop. Proceed to thread the third loop through the second and so on until the last loop is secured around the button (Figure 113).

The slits for slash pockets can be woven on the loom too if they fall vertically on the warp (Figure 114). Plan the position

142

of the pocket, transfer the placement to the loom and weave a corresponding slit. The slit can later have a pocket sewn behind it and even a needle woven welt for the slit edge (see Seams).

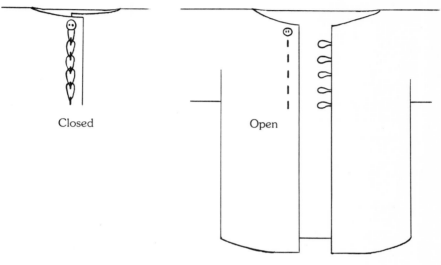

Closed   Open

113. Slits, loops and button

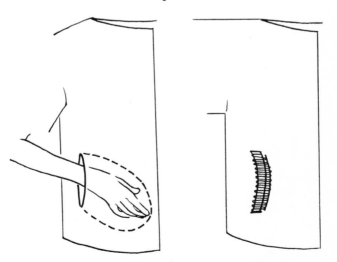

Planning Pocket Inside of Slit   Woven Pocket Welt Attached to Slit

114. Slit pocket

To design an appropriate pocket to place behind the slit, with the garment on, place your hand flat inside the slit and mark its position with pins. From these marks make a pocket pattern allowing ¾" seam allowances and cut two pieces of lining for each pocket. Sew around the curved edges from seam allowance to seam allowance (Figure 115). Fold back one of the straight edges and slip stitch these pocket lining edges to the slit edges.

Fringe can be woven on the selvedge edges producing, along with the warp fringe, four fringed edges. This is a great touch for a pillow or shawl. Before the weaving begins, decide on the length of fringe desired and use this length as a measure to place a string through the reed on each side of the warp to be fringed. Attach the strings to the back and breast beams. The weaving progresses by passing two shots just to the selvedges and the next two shots out around the strings. Cut the weft fringe away from the string when the loops reach the front beam. The web produced has secure selvedges and fringe as well (Figure 116).

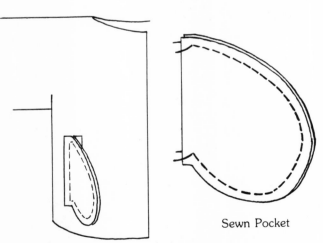

Sewn Pocket

Sewn Pocket Attached to Wrong Side of Pocket Slit

115. Cut and sew pocket

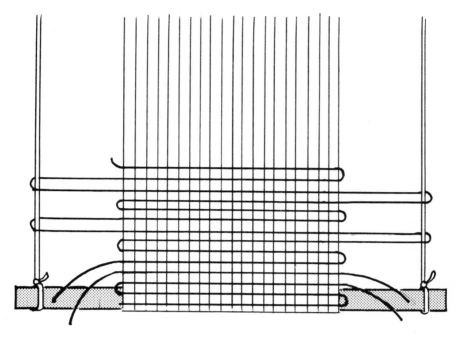

116. Selvedge fringe

Fringes can be woven separately on the loom. These strips
of fringe are woven in pairs by threading two narrow, closely
sett, twill theaded warps each ½" to 3" wide and placed 2" to
10" apart in the reed. The weft should be a decorative material
and the shuttle used should be longer than the distance between the warp sections. The weaving begins at the left edge
by passing the shuttle all the way across both warp sections.
Then two picks are woven in the right hand warp. The third
shot travels across both warps and is followed by two picks in
the left warp. Before the weaving passes around the cloth
beam, the weft between the woven strips is cut up the middle
(Figure 117).

145

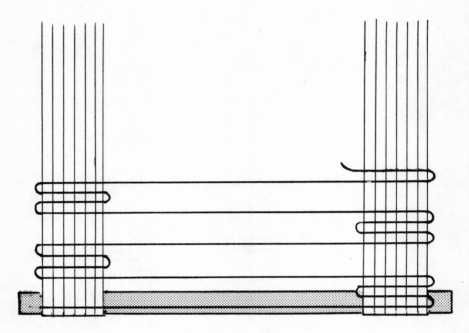

117. Woven fringe

Stop the Weft

When the web is removed from the loom, the most important consideration is keeping the weft in place. For yard goods merely machine stitch along the raw edge using two rows of small, straight stitches or one row of zig-zag stitches as an overcast.

The overhand knot is the most common warp finish and, in most cases, the best and simplest solution to the finishing problem. To tie the knot, form a loop in the strands being tied and pass the ends of the strands over and through the loop (Figure 10). While pulling gently on the strands, push the knot up against the cloth. For overhand knots that won't push up against the cloth, obtain a tight finish by tying a half knot first to take the pressure off the overhand knot being manipulated.

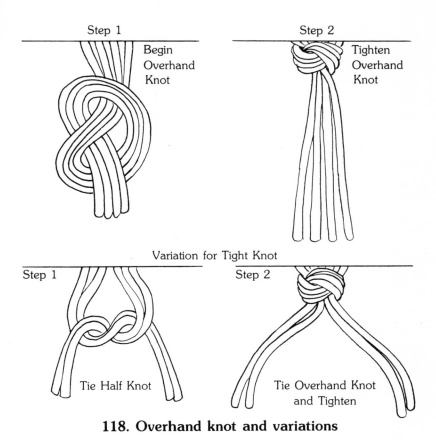

Begin
Overhand
Knot

Tighten
Overhand
Knot

Variation for Tight Knot

Step 1

Step 2

Tie Half Knot

Tie Overhand Knot
and Tighten

118. Overhand knot and variations

Overhand knots on strong warps can also be tightened by separating the ends below the knot into two equal groups and pulling the groups in opposite directions (Figure 118).

A clever but easy variation on the overhand knot stops the warp from pulling together and prevents the weft from drooping between knots. Working from left to right, select a group of ends to make an overhand knot. Beginning at the left edge, drop the right hand thread from the group and, instead, pick up the adjoining left thread from the next knot's group making sure that these two threads form a cross that holds the weft in place. Proceed to tie the overhand knot in the usual fashion.

Start the next knot including the dropped right-hand end from the first knot (Figure 119).

A flat variation of the overhand knot suffices to finish informal place mats and other utilitarian pieces that need a knotted finish without knot bumps. To tie the flat knot, select a normal group of ends for a knot and separate the edge thread. Pass this thread around the group and down through the loop created. Push the knot up and tighten it by pulling on the one end involved in the knot (Figure 120).

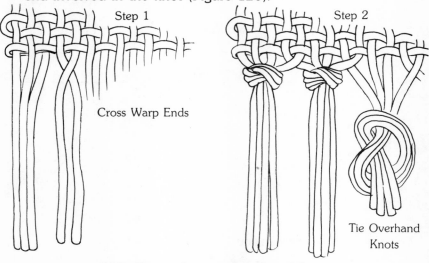

Step 1

Cross Warp Ends

Step 2

Tie Overhand Knots

119. Crossed warp overhand knot

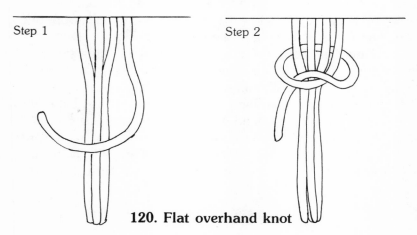

Step 1

Step 2

120. Flat overhand knot

There are exceptions to the general use of the overhand knot. Both warp-faced and weft-faced fabrics need a different treatment for the opposite reasons. Skinny warp overhand knots at the edge of a tapestry seldom add to a tapestry design. There are literally hundreds of knots, braids, stitches, chainings, bindings and supplementary weaves that can be used to finish weft-faced webs but simply threading the ends back into the weaving produces a firm edged clean finish, holds the weft in place and protects the warp from wear.

Depending on the density of the tapestry or rug, each end may be threaded back into the cloth by using a blunt tapestry needle to work each warp in with the next end for 1" or 2" (Figure 121). For extremely tight tapestries, only every other end should be threaded back into the weaving to prevent puckering. Once these ends are threaded back into the weaving, the tapestry should be extremely firm securing all of the ends. Both the threaded and unthreaded ends can then be trimmed close to the weaving.

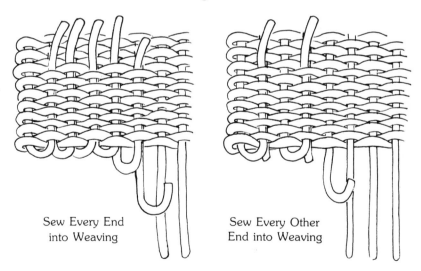

Sew Every End
into Weaving

Sew Every Other
End into Weaving

121. Ends threaded back into the weaving

Overhand knots are not a suitable finish for warp-faced weaves because the density of the warp makes it impossible to tie an even row of knots without distorting the cloth. Again, a variety of excellent solutions are available. A favorite solution for a decorative warp-faced piece is to square-knot one pair of warp ends, skip up to an inch of ends, and repeat the process across the width of the unfinished edge. Remember, the square knot is a right over left half knot followed by a left over right half knot (Figure 11). The square knot is used rather than an overhand knot because it better simulates the natural puffiness of the warp (Figure 122). The effect is an almost invisible finish.

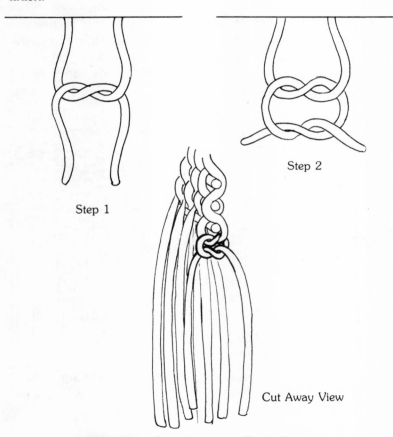

Step 1

Step 2

Cut Away View

122. Warp-faced square knot finish

The Neolithic knot, also known as the vertical half hitch, is one of the few finishes that reduces the bulk of the warp while securing the weft and is, therefore, perfectly suited to warp-faced weaving. Working left to right, begin the knots by laying a butterfly of the knotting yarn over the group of warp ends to be bound together. Pass the butterfly under the group of threads from right to left: then bring it over the starting end of the knot, traveling diagonally to the right. Again pass the butterfly under the group from right to left and then bring it simultaneously over the group of warp threads and under the previously formed diagonal. Tighten the knot formed, and proceed to the next group of warp ends being careful not to pull one knot too close to the next one (Figure 123A and B).

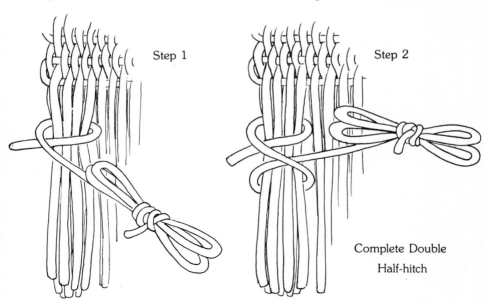

Step 1

Step 2

Complete Double
Half-hitch

Pass Butterfly around
Group of Ends

123A. Neolithic knot

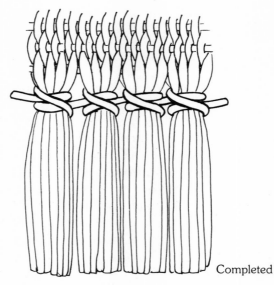

Completed

123B. Neolithic knot

Embellished Edges

Many weavings need fringed and decorated edges to complete the design. Plain woven stoles in particular benefit from a lacy fringe.

The easiest fringe is one produced by the original overhand knots. To trim the fringe, place the weaving flat on a table and position it so that the knotted edge is the desired fringe length from the table edge. Place a weighted board on the weaving and comb the fringe over the edge of the table. Then, holding the fringe in place with one hand, trim the ends using the table edge as a guide.

A more intricate fringe is created by separating the ends in the original knots into two equal groups and to combine the groups of ends from adjacent knots by using overhand knots. These alternating knots are worked across the warp; omit the outside group of ends on each edge. A third row of overhand knots using the original combination of ends catches the outside groups thus finishing the process (Figure 124).

152

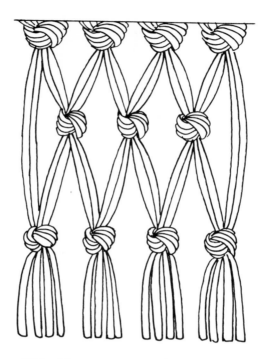

124. Alternating overhand knots

Another related fringe uses the same knot and the same idea of dividing the ends in each overhand knot into two groups, but adjacent groups are not tied together. Rather, beginning at the left edge, the left group from the first knot is tied to the left groups of the second and third knots. The right group of the first knot is woven over and under the tied groups from the second and third knots and tied to the left group of the fourth knot. From here the pattern repeats; the right group of the second knot is woven through and tied to the left group of the fifth knot. In turn, the next right group is woven through and tied to a left group three knots away. The fringe is completed by tying the remaining three right groups together (Figure 125).

125. Interlacing overhand knots

Fringe can be attached to a finished selvedge using a crochet hook to pull loops of yarn through the cloth. The fringe is fastened by passing the ends through the loop forming a lark's head (Figure 126).

Tassels applied to corners or along knotted edges add design emphasis by providing color, texture and movement. Begin a tassel by winding a number of loops of yarn a little longer than the length of the tassel. Fasten the loops either with a length of string or with the knotted warp ends of a weaving. Smooth the loops and secure them with a binding around the top of the bundle.

A self finishing binding is good for this job. To make a 1" binding, cut a 16" to 20" length of yarn. Fold back 4" on one end and hold this loop against the bundle to be bound.

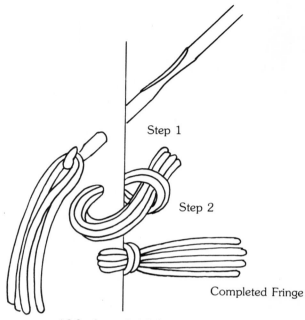

Step 1

Step 2

Completed Fringe

126. Attached fringe

Beginning 1″ from the short end, carefully wrap up toward the loop. When the binding is done, pull the wrapping thread through the loop and pull on the exposed botton end of the loop. When the loop disappears into the wrapping, pull on both ends to tighten the wrap, then trim both ends flush (Figure 127).

Plying is a neat finish for bulky materials. It is appropriate for card and inkle weaves as well as for thick blankets. Using two groups of threads spin both groups clockwise and then ply them together counterclockwise. With a little practice to coordinate the simultaneous clockwise twists, this goes along rapidly. Although plying holds itself together, a finishing overhand knot is advisable for slippery yarns.

Plaiting is better for heavy use such as rug edges. Three strand flat braid is the most familiar. Holding three groups of yarn, begin by bringing the right yarn over the middle yarn.

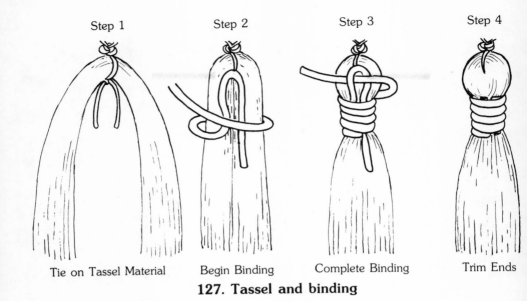

Step 1	Step 2	Step 3	Step 4
Tie on Tassel Material	Begin Binding	Complete Binding	Trim Ends

127. Tassel and binding

The left yarn crosses the new middle yarn followed again by the right yarn and so on. The braid is finished with an overhand knot or a binding.

Four strand round braid, frequently used as two tone shoulder straps for Greek bags, is a durable construction for weight bearing, decorative ropes. Holding four strands or four groups of threads, cross the center threads right over left. Now begin plaiting by passing the right hand strand to the left under the cross, up and to the right over one strand. The left strand then travels under the new cross to the right, up and to the left over one strand. The two plaiting steps are repeated until the braid is the desired length (Figure 128).

Basic hems are ho-hum but, with a little added imagination, they add emphasis to an edge. Try turning a hem to the outside and stitching it down with chain or feather stitches. A rolled hem, rather than retreating, can be rolled around cording and overcast with a heavy yarn to produce a stiff and decorative edge. Using a variety of yarns and stitches for the overcasting increases the design possibilities.

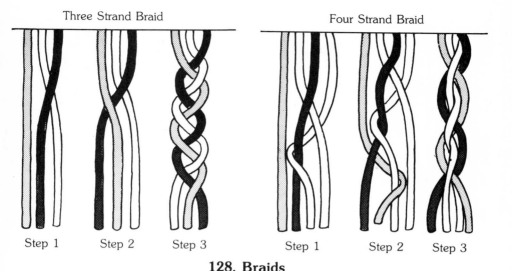

Three Strand Braid   Four Strand Braid

Step 1   Step 2   Step 3   Step 1   Step 2   Step 3

128. Braids

Seams

Whether invisible or decorative, seams are necessary for the best appearance of the finished product. Invisible seams are necessary to join weaving sections into a planned, overall design. Tightly woven tapestries, done in sections, may be joined in the same manner as Gobelin tapestry slits. Using a tapestry needle threaded with a weft colored thread, bring the needle up through a selvedge weft loop inside the edge warp. Pass the thread over and down through the corresponding loop and the edge warp of the adjoining tapestry section. Proceed to the next stitch creating a slight diagonal line on the back of the work.

A truly invisible seam can be made in a slightly loose tapestry by alternately picking up a warp from each edge using a tapestry needle threaded with sturdy warp yarn. Every inch or two, pull the sewing yarn very hard, forcing the loops together (Figure 129). Similarly, balanced fabrics can be joined by alternately picking up weft loops inside the first warp thread. This type of seam is also used for joining knits (Figure 130).

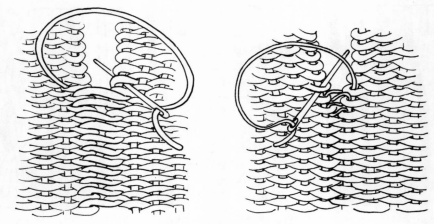

129. Tapestry seams

130. Narrow seam

The figure eight stitch creates a double ridge mimicking applied trims. Worked in a variety of colors as the Guatemalan weavers do, attractive bands are created. Select contrasting colors of a lustrous floss or 2-ply wool. Begin by pushing the threaded needle up through the first selvedge ¼" to ½" from the edge. Bring the yarn over that selvedge and under the adjoining cloth. To complete the stitch, bring the needle up through the second selvedge ¼" to ½" from the edge, over that selvedge and back under the first selvedge. Sew the seam with stripes of various colored yarns for added interest.

By elongating the figure eight stitch a completely different effect results. Called the ancient stitch or baseball stitch, it is a perfect seam for things like ponchos (Figure 131).

All sorts of embroidery stitches can be used to join two woven edges. Even band weaving can be used to join two woven edges with the added benefit of an extra inch which can save a too-narrow weaving. Warp an appropriate band and thread a rigid heddle or card weaving set-up to create the shed. Use a back strap system to apply tension to the threaded band weaving. Then, using a threaded tapestry needle for a shuttle, go through the band weaving shed and pick up a weft loop behind the edge warp of one selvedge. Change the shed and, returning the needle, pick up a weft loop and warp thread from the second selvedge being joined. For coarse bands being combined with finer fabrics, pick up both selvedges in each shed.

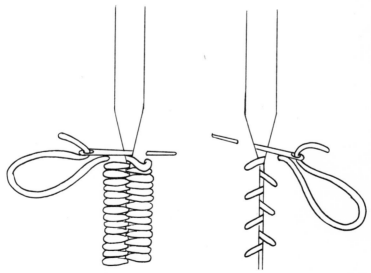

131. Figure eight (left) and ancient stitch (right)

The same band weaving setup can also be used to finish warp ends with the warp ends used as weft in the band weaving. Weave each end across the band and back into the next shed, producing two crossing wefts in each shed (Figure 132).

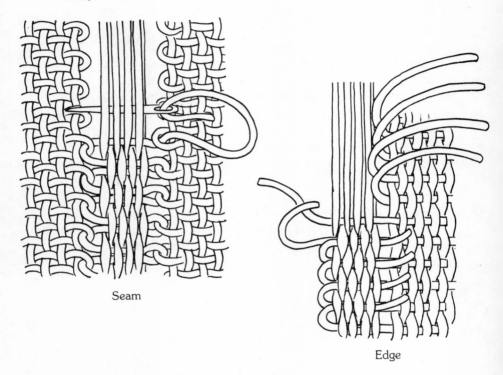

Seam

Edge

132. Band woven seam and edge

Buttons and Frogs

Buttons can be purchased in a wide variety of shapes, sizes and materials. Bone, wood, mother-of-pearl, even nut shells and peach pits can be carved into buttons. Buttons can be made by covering purchased button forms following manufacturers directions. Buttons can be crocheted or knotted. Basket-ry techniques can be used to produce attractive discs to be used as buttons. Beads can be used as buttons. Ball buttons can be made out of monkey fist knots formed around wooden beads.

The monkey's fist develops in three stages. First, the tying cord is secured by the left thumb and wound three times around a "V" formed by the index and second finger of the left hand. The cord is then turned at a right angle and wound three times around the original wrappings, passing the cord between the index and second fingers. Secure the wrapping cord by passing it through the opening held by the index finger. At this point, the knot is slipped from the fingers and a small bead is inserted as a hard center. The final wrapping goes through the opening left by the fingers and is also wound around three times. The slack from the loops originally on the fingers is worked out methodically by first taking the slack out of the last big loop to be formed. Then the slack is adjusted out of the next to the last loop formed and finally the slack is removed from the original loop. Larger monkey's fist knots can be formed by increasing the windings in each stage to four or even five passes (Figure 133).

By adding a carrick bend, sailor talk for a sensuous knot that weavers call a Josephine, to the existing monkey's fist, a delightful frog results. The Josephine develops by turning an end-under loop in the left cord. Placing the right cord over the left cord loop, proceed with the right cord under the under end and over the over cord of the left loop. The right cord then travels under the left cord loop, over itself and under the left loop again. The knot is completed by tucking the ends back into the knot (Figure 134).

For a more intricate effect follow each thread of the knot back around, through all the overs and unders, to the beginning of the knot forming a double strand knot. Finally, the other side of the frog is made by omitting the monkey's fist and beginning the Josephine with a loop.

Step 1

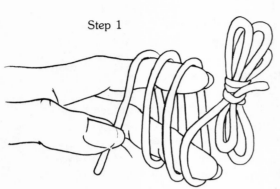

Wrap Cord Butterfly Vertically
around Fingers Three Times

Step 2

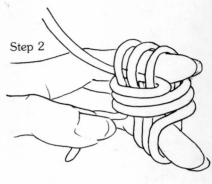

Wrap Cord Three Times Horizontally
between Fingers and Pass Cord
through Vertical Wrappings

Step 3

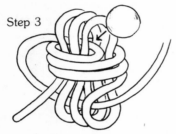

Insert Bead into Center of Knot

Step 4

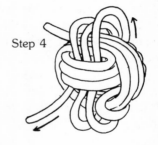

Completely Enclose Bead with Three
Wrappings and Tighten Knot

Completed Three Pass Knot

Five Pass Variation

133. Monkey's fist

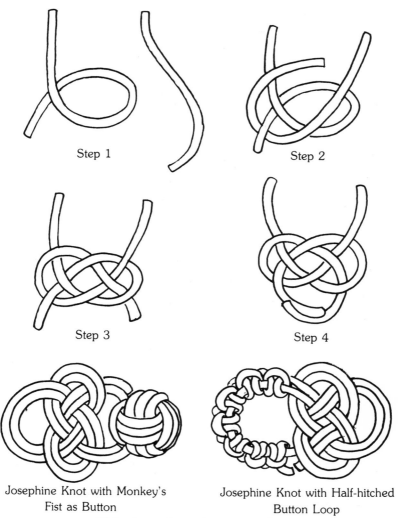

Step 1

Step 2

Step 3

Step 4

Josephine Knot with Monkey's
Fist as Button

Josephine Knot with Half-hitched
Button Loop

134. Josephine knot and frog

Hangings and Installations

Hanging devices, like finishes, should be considered in the design stage. Interesting things happen when the installation is considered along with the design.

Occasionally, an unusual hanging device, even some found object, is the beginning of a piece. In this case it is important to integrate the weaving and the object. One of the best solutions is to weave it in. Plan the weaving to proceed from bottom to top. When the time comes to include the hanging device, build any necessary weft shapes to accommodate the shape of the hanging device. Weave in the object and build more weft around it to secure its position. If the hanging device can be drilled the weaving can be knotted in place after the piece is off the loom.

For concealed rods, simply hem or face the weaving and slide the rod through the resulting casing. When a fringe is desired at the top of a hanging, knot the fringe and turn the hem and fringe to the front of the piece.

Woven and hemmed tabs allow a beautiful bar to show through. Wrapping groups of warp ends into loops accomplishes the same thing.

So often it is the hanging or installation that gives away the amateur. Generally the more complicated and prominent the hanging device, the more it detracts from the weaving. Heavy frames in particular seem out of place. Since a weaving isn't a painting, the frame serves no structural purpose and must, therefore, be considered as a design element only.

However, the "see-thru" frame, consisting of a shallow plexiglas box and a slip-fit, white cardboard box, solves the problem of how to display fragments and studies. Simply arrange the fragment on the carboard box and, if necessary, pin it in place with stainless steel silk pins. Slip on the plexiglas box, hang it up and enjoy.

Well-designed tapestries with clean edges should be displayed with as little obtrusive hardware as possible. A casing made of rug binding can be slip stitched to the top of the tapestry to carry a curtain rod. A favorite finish for larger works is to slip stitch a 6" wide strip of canvas or denim which is 3" longer than the tapestry width, to the top of the tapestry back. Cut a length of 1" × 2" clear pine ¼" shorter than the tapestry width. Sand the corners and edges. Lay the tapestry face down on a flat surface with the canvas strip extended. Place a 1″ edge of the 1″ × 2″ on the canvas strip flush with the slip stitched seam. Wrap the cloth around the wood and staple it to what will be the inside of the wood assembly. Fold the wood down flush to the tapestry. Screw two eye hooks to the top of the wood through the canvas. The wood holds the tapestry out from the wall and creates dramatic shadows (Figure 135A and B).

For a quick solution to tapestry dispay, sew lengths of warp material along the weft ridges on the back of the tapestry, and tie these strings to a flat piece of wood. The strings should be placed near the edge of the tapestry every 2″ or 3″ for a secure and ripple free installation (Figure 136).

Step 1   Step 2

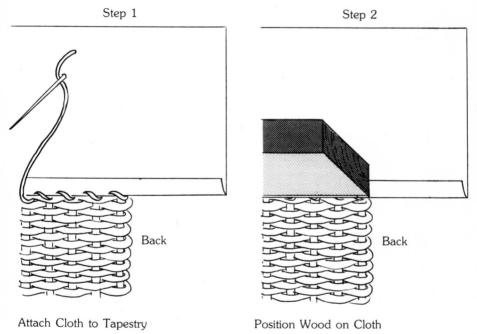

Back   Back

Attach Cloth to Tapestry   Position Wood on Cloth

135A. Hanging a tapestry

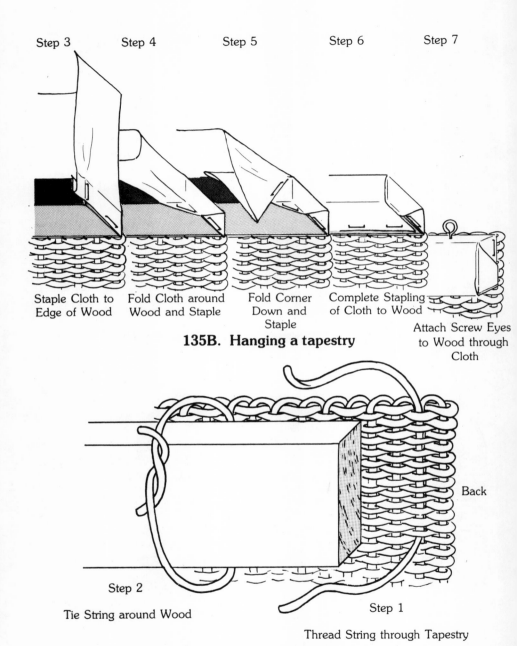

Step 3   Step 4   Step 5   Step 6   Step 7

Staple Cloth to   Fold Cloth around   Fold Corner   Complete Stapling
Edge of Wood   Wood and Staple   Down and   of Cloth to Wood
                                   Staple

Attach Screw Eyes
to Wood through
Cloth

135B. Hanging a tapestry

Back

Step 2

Tie String around Wood

Step 1

Thread String through Tapestry

136. Tie on a hanging device

166

Appendix I:

Coming to Terms

One of the biggest secrets of weaving seems to be terminology. Not only does spelling change; meanings vary, with some terms having several, somewhat contradictory meanings. The following glossary should suffice for conversations with most American weavers.

Accidental: Referring to the speckled area in four block, four-harness overshot.

Apron: Canvas fabric attached to the cloth and warp beams used to connect the warp to the beams.

Back beam: Fixed member at the back of the loom over which the warp passes.

Back stitch: 1. A needlework technique in which the needle travels through the cloth in the opposite direction to the progressing stitches; 2. Any technique where a thread travels in a direction opposite to the progress of the work (e.g., soumak, Brook's bouquet).

Backstrap: A primitive tensioning method employing a fixed object and the weaver's body to stretch the warp.

Back-to-front: See *Front-to-back.*

Balanced weave: 1. A weave in which the ends per inch are equal to the picks per inch; 2. A weave in which half of the warp threads are raised for each shot.

Ball winder: A machine for producing pull-string balls of yarn.

Basket weave: A weave in which the same two (or more) warp ends alternate with two (or more) weft picks.

Batten: See *Beater.*

Beam: Any of a number of horizontal loom parts that support the warp.

Beaming: The process of winding the warp onto the warp beam.

Beater: The frame containing the reed, used to strike the fell.

Bight: A group of warp ends treated alike, usually ready for tying.

Block: 1. A pattern unit or section of a weave; 2. Blocking, a finishing process using water or steam to control the shape of the finished product.

Boat shuttle: A tapered device containing a bobbin and used to carry the weft through the shed.

Bobbin: A reel or spool to carry thread; a spool or quill mounted in a shuttle.

Bobbin winder: A tool for preparing wound spools or quills of yarn.

Boucle yarn: A novelty yarn with a characteristic looped element.

Braiding: A plaiting technique with oblique interlacements of elements.

Breast beam: Fixed member at the front of the loom over which the warp passes.

Brocade: A three-element fabric based on plain weave with an additional decorative surface element.

Butterfly: A bundle of yarn wound around the fingers, secured at the center and used as a bobbin in tapestry and finger weaves.

168

Cable: Two or more plied yarns twisted together.

Cape: Side upright of a loom which supports the castle.

Card weaving: 1. A weaving process based on cards with holes in the corners which take the place of harnesses; 2. A narrow band of weaving produced by using weaving cards.

Cartoon: A drawing used as a guide for weaving especially in tapestry.

Castle: The central piece across the top of the loom from which jacks or harnesses are hung.

Chain: 1. The interlooped warp after it has been removed from the warping reel; 2. Chaining, to remove the warp from the reel by interlooping; 3. Referring to the treadling draft.

Chenille: A cut pile yarn.

Choke: A tie around the warp as it comes from the reel used to prevent tangles.

Cloth beam: Horizontal, rotating loom part around which the finished cloth is wound.

Colonial overshot: A family of traditional American weaves characterized by complex patterns created by wool floats on a cotton or linen ground.

Cord: 1. See *Cable;* 2. Fabric with warp or weft ribs.

Corduroy: A weave with long floats which are cut to produce a pile surface.

Counterbalance loom: A loom action based on balanced sinking and rising harnesses.

Counter march loom: A loom action based on independent rising and sinking harnesses.

Creel: See *Reel* or *Spool rack.*

Crepe: A weave or fabric with a mottled or crinkled surface.

Cross: The crossing of threads at the start of a warp which preserves the order of the ends.

Cut: 1. Small skein or part of a skein; 2. A unit of measure of chenille; 3. A unit of measure of wool where 300 yards in a pound equals 1 cut.

Danish medallion: A weft technique creating a looped stitch on the surface of the fabric.

Denier: A unit of size of filament yarns where 900 meters equals 1 gram.

Dent: One space in a reed.

Design: 1. The arrangement of elements to develop a motif; 2. Complete weaving directions including the materials, draft and pattern.

Double weave: An interlacement that produces two distinct layers of cloth.

Dobby: 1. A loom using a mechanized system to produce a treadling pattern; 2. Any of the small pattern weaves characteristic of the process.

Dog: Braking mechanism for a rachet.

Draft: 1. The threading plan, the threading and treadling used to produce a weave; 2. The process of planning a weave on graph paper.

Draw: The threading pattern.

Draw-down: Graphed drawing of the interlacement of threads.

Draw loom: A manually operated complex loom capable of intricate designs.

Dressing: 1. Preparing the loom for weaving; 2. Preparation applied to the warp to facilitate weaving.

Dukagång: Swedish inlay technique based on a regular 3 thread float.

End: Warp thread.

Entering: Threading the heddles and sleying the reed.

Embroidery: Needlework applied to a fabric.

Fell: The edge of a web formed by the last shot beaten in place.

Felt: 1. A non-woven fabric made of fibers pressed together by heat, moisture and friction; 2. To cause a fabric to shrink and mat.

Filler: See *Weft*.

Flake yarn: A yarn with pieces of loosely attached fibers.

Flat shuttle: A long polished stick with notched ends, used to carry weft.

Float: Portion of a warp or weft yarn passing over two or more of the opposite set of yarns.

Flossa: See *Rya*.

Fly shuttle: A mechanical device mounted on the beater; automatically puts a specially weighted shuttle through the shed.

Fork: A tined tool used to beat tapestry weft.

Frame loom: A simple weaving device based on a rectangular structure which holds the warp taut.

Front-to-back: (cf., back-to-front) 1. An indication that the harness nearest the weaver is treated as the first harness; 2. Threading the loom first and then winding the warp.

Ghiordes: See *Rya knot*.

Grist: Size of thread.

Ground work: Plain weave web on which pattern is superimposed.

Guide string: A cord used to place the warp correctly on the warping frame.

Hand: The feel or texture of a cloth.

Hank: A unit of measure for cotton and wool; a hank of cotton equals 840 yards; a hank of worsted equals 560 yards; and a hank of woolen equals 300 yards.

Harness: Frames that hold a group of heddles on the loom.

Heading: Narrow band of rags, reeds or heavy rug yarn at the beginning of a weaving.

Heddle, Heald: A wire, metal or string device with an opening through which the ends are passed.

Heddle frame: See *Harness*.

Heddle gauge: Jig for tying string heddles.

Heddle hook: A tool for threading the warp ends through the heddle eyes.

Heddle horse: A device used to balance pairs of harnesses on a four-harness counterbalance loom.

Hemstitching: Needlework technique used to secure the weft at the edge of a web.

Herringbone: A twill derivative weave.

Hombre: A yarn that creates an irregular color arrangement.

Ikat: A process of selectively dying portions of warp or weft before weaving.

Inkle loom: A simple weaving device for producing narrow, warp-faced bands.

Inlay: Discontinuous weft yarns added to create design motif.

Jack: Lifting mechanism on a jack loom.

Jack loom: A loom action based on independent rising harnesses.

Jacquard loom: A complex loom capable of producing intricate patterns.

Jaspé: See *Ikat*.

Kilim: A form of slit tapestry.

Lace weave: A web characterized by warp and weft distortion and/or spaced warp and weft.

Laith: See *Beater*.

Lam, Lamm: Horizontal loom parts attached to the center of the harnesses and tied to the treadles to insure level harness action.

Lark's head: A knot used in macramé and loom tying.

Lary sticks: Supports for the reed and lease sticks; used while dressing the loom.

Lease, Leash: See *Cross*.

Lease sticks, Leash sticks: A pair of thin strips of wood used to hold the cross in the warp.

Leno: A lace weave characterized by pairs or groups of crossing weft threads secured with weft.

Line: A form of linen with fibers longer than 12".

Linsey-woolsey: Fabric woven with a linen warp and a wool weft.

Loom: Any of a number of devices that produce woven goods.

Loom waste: That portion of the warp remaining on the loom when the weaving is finished; thrums.

Mail: The eye of a string heddle.

Marches: See *Lams*

Mercerize: To apply a finish to cotton or worsted to improve its luster and strength.

172

Metallic yarn: Any yarn of or looking like metal; mylar.

Mohair: Yarn made from the hair of the Angora goat.

Multiharness: Having more than four harnesses.

Neolithic knot: Double half hitch, used to secure warp ends.

Niddy noddy: Hand reel for winding skeins.

Norwegian shuttle: A small flat shuttle with a tapered edge used as a beater for band weaving.

Novelty yarn: Any yarn with variations of size, color, twist or fiber.

Opposite, On opposites: 1. Weaving patterns that contain no accidentals; 2. Four-harness weaving patterns threaded in two exclusive blocks.

Overshot: A weave characterized by weft floats.

Paddle: A flat tool with rows of holes or slots; used to warp several threads at once.

Pattern: The decorative figure in a weave.

Pawl: See *Dog.*

Pick: 1. A single shot of weft; 2. Picking, the act of passing the weft through the shed.

Pickup stick: A slender, pointed tool used to lift groups of warp ends.

Pile weave: A web characterized by weft loops or knots creating a textured surface.

Plain weave: A common weave created by alternately interlacing warp and weft, usually producing a balanced weave.

Plaiting: A technique of oblique interlacements of elements; braiding.

Poke shuttle: See *Flat shuttle.*

Ply: Referring to the strands in a yarn.

Profile draft: See *Short draft.*

Quill: A tube around which weft is wound.

Race: A flat cross piece on the lower front of the beater used to support the shuttle.

Rack: A frame to hold spools or cones.

Raddle: A device for spreading the warp when dressing the loom.

Raffia: A natural fiber from the palm, *Raphia ruffia*.

Ramie: A natural fiber similar to linen.

Rachet: The circular, toothed part of a loom brake.

Reed: A regular, comb-like device used to position the warp and weft.

Reed hook: A tool used to pull the warp through the reed.

Reel: A rotating device used to facilitate warping.

Rep: A weave with warp of weft ribs.

Rigid heddle: A frame with holes and slots; it serves as a shed device and reed on certain simple looms.

Rising shed: See *Jack loom.*

Roller: The upper cross-piece of a counterbalance loom from which the harnesses are hung.

Roving: Strands of untwisted material loosely held together.

Rosepath: A common threading producing variations of a diamond and dot pattern.

Rya, Ryijy: A knot used to produce a pile surface.

Satin: A weave characterized by a lustrous surface composed of floats.

Sectional beam: A warp beam divided into 2″ sections used for sectional warping where groups of warp are wound directly onto the beam.

Selvedge, Selvage: The woven edge of the web.

Sett, Set: 1. The number of warp ends per inch; 2. The number of dents per inch in a reed.

Shed: 1. A space created in the warp through which the weft travels; 2. Shedding: The process of raising and/or lowering the harnesses.

Shed sticks: See *Lease sticks.*

Short draft: The blocks of a pattern, omitting the threadings.

Shot: A passing of the weft through the shed.

Shuttle: A tool for carrying weft thread through the shed.

Shuttle race: See *Race.*

Single: Yarn composed of one strand.

Sinker: Harness that moves down to create a shed.

Sinking shed: See counterbalance, sinkers.

Sizing: A finish that adds body to yarns or fabric.

Skein: Yarn wound and secured into a large, orderly loop.

Skeleton tie-up: One harness tied to one treadle.

Ski shuttle: A long shuttle with the weft wound around curved ends protruding from the flat bottom; used in rug weaving.

Slab beam, Slab stock: 1. See *Back beam;* 2. See *Warp beam.*

Sley: To draw the warp ends through the dents in the reed.

Slit: A vertical opening in a tapestry; caused by the meeting of two pattern areas.

Slot: See *Dent.*

Slub: A yarn with bulky, unspun areas.

Soumak: A low-pile technique producing a ridge by back stitching.

Snitch: A combination of a lark's head and square knot used to tie lams to treadles.

Spanish lace: A technique in which small, adjoining areas of warp are woven with a continuous weft.

Spool rack: A device for holding put-up yarn.

Spreader: See *Raddle.*

Square knot: A macramé knot also used in loom tying.

Squirrel cage reel: A device for holding large skeins.

Stretcher: See *Temple.*

Swift: A device for holding a skein as it is wound onto shuttles or into balls.

Tabby: 1. See *Plain Weave;* 2. Plain weave used between pattern shots.

Tabby shed: Treadling which brings up every other warp thread.

Takeup: The amount of yarn lost to the interlacement of the web.

Tapestry: A weft-faced plain weave usually decorative with discontinuous weft areas.

Tapestry fork: A tool used as a beater for tapestry.

Tapestry loom: A two-harness loom used specifically for tapestries and rugs.

Tease: To raise the nap of a fabric, usually by brushing.

Temple: A device placed across the web near the fell to prevent the cloth from pulling in.

Tension: The tautness of the warp yarns on the loom.

Textile: 1. A construction made of fibers; 2. Woven goods.

Texture: See *Hand*.

Throw shuttle: See *Boat shuttle*.

Thrums: The portion of the warp yarn which cannot be woven.

Tie-up: The connection of the harnesses to the treadles.

Top castle: See *Castle*.

Tow: A form of linen containing short fibers.

Treadle, pedal: 1. A lever that controls the harnesses; 2. The act of depressing the lever.

Tromp as writ: Treadling corresponds to the threading.

Tubular double weave: An interlacement of warp and weft producing two layers of cloth connected at the selvedges.

Twill: A family of weaves characterized by diagonal lines.

Twining: A two-element weft construction characterized by the wefts twisting around each other as they interlace with the warp.

Umbrella swift: See *Swift*.

Unbalanced weave: The opposite of a balanced weave, with either more weft or more warp exposed. See *Warp-face* and *Weft-face*.

Warp: The threads stretched on the loom.

Warp beam: The horizontal loom member below the back beam; tensions and stores the warp.

Warp-face: A weave in which the warp predominates.

Warping: Preparing lengths of yarn to be placed on the loom as warp.

Warp hook: See *Heddle hook*.

Warping board: A frame with pegs mounted at intervals; used to prepare warps.

Warping comb: See *Raddle*.

Warping creel: See *Warping reel*.

Warping paddle: See *Paddle.*

Warping reel: A rotating device used to facilitate warp winding.

Warp-weighted loom: A weaving device with tension provided by hanging weights.

Weave: The interlacement of warp and weft.

Weaver's knot: A non-slipping tie.

Web: Fabric created by weaving.

Weft: Threads interlaced with the warp to produce a web.

Wheel: See *Rachet.*

Whip beam: See *Warp beam.*

Woof: See *Weft.*

Woolen: 1. Homespun; 2. A wool yarn spun of fleece with coarser, shorter staple than worsted.

Worsted: A wool yarn spun of fleece with longer, smoother staple than homespun.

Yarn count: The relative size of yarns measured by a variety of systems.

Appendix II:

Parts of a Loom

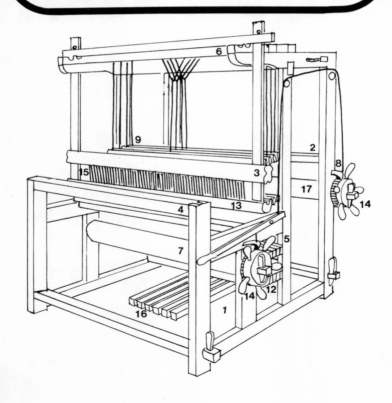

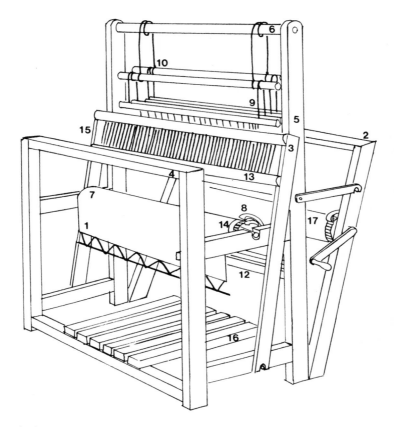

1. Apron
2. Back beam
3. Beater
4. Breast beam
5. Cape
6. Castle
7. Cloth beam
8. Dog
9. Harness
10. Heddle horse
11. Jack
12. Lam
13. Race
14. Rachet
15. Reed
16. Treadle
17. Warp beam

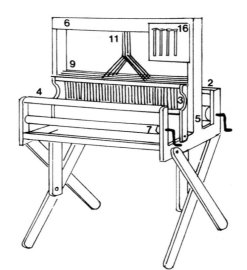

Appendix III:

Metric Conversions

1 meter = 1.094 yards
1 yard = 0.9144 meters

1 kilogram = 2.205 pounds
1 pound = 0.435 kilograms

1 centimeter = 0.3937 inches
1 inch = 2.54 centimeters

Bibliography

Atwater, Mary M. *Byways in Handweaving*. New York: The Macmillan Company, 1967.

———. *The Shuttlecraft Book of American Handweaving*. New York: The Macmillan Company, 1956.

Baizerman, Suzanne and Searle, Karen. *Finishes in the Ethnic Tradition*. St. Paul, Minn.: Dos Tejedores, 1978.

Black, Mary E. *New Key to Weaving*. Milwaukee, Wis.: Bruce Publishing Company, 1957.

Brostoff, Laya. "Winding a Bobbin." *Shuttle, Spindle and Dyepot,* volume IX #1, issue 33, Winter 1977, pp. 73–75.

Carlson, Estelle. "Adapting Inkle Patterns to Wider Width." *Shuttle, Spindle and Dyepot,* volume VIII #1, issue 29, Winter 1976, pp. 87–91.

181

Chetwynd, Hilary. *Simple Weaving.* New York: Watson-Guptill Publications, 1969.

Collingwood, Peter. *The Techniques of Rug Weaving.* New York: Watson-Guptill Publications, 1968.

Davison, Marguerite P. *A Handweaver's Pattern Book.* Swarthmore, Pa.: M. P. Davison, 1963.

DePeaux, Barbara and Tyler, Mary. "Bands to Broadloom." *Shuttle, Spindle and Dyepot,* volume VIII #1, issue 29, Winter 1976, pp. 86–87, 89–91.

Ekman, Erne and Spangle, Richard. "Countermarch Explained." *Looms & Yarns.* Berea, Ohio, 1976.

Emery, Irene. *Primary Structures of Fabrics.* Washington, D.C.: The Textile Museum, 1966.

Fiberarts. Bi-monthly. Asheville, N.C.

Groff, Russell E. *Card Weaving.* Robin and Russ Handweavers. McMinnville, Or.

Warp and Weft. Monthly bulletin. Robin and Russ Handweavers. McMinnville, Or.

Handweaver & Craftman. Periodical (out of print—available through libraries). New York.

Harvey, Virginia I. *Macramé, The Art of Creative Knotting.* New York: Van Nostrand Reinhold Company, 1967.

Held, Shirley E. *Weaving, A Handbook for Fiber Craftsmen.* New York: Holt Rinehart and Winston Inc., 1973.

Helps and Hints, Compiled by Handweavers Guild of America, Inc., Service Committee, West Hartford, Conn.

Howard, Margaret. "Analysis Based on Warp Threads." *Shuttle, Spindle and Dyepot,* volume III #2, Spring 1972, p. 13.

Oelsner, G. H. *Handbook of Weavers.* New York: Dover Publications Inc., 1952.

Pierucci, Louise, "An Introduction to Tapestry." *Shuttle, Spindle and Dyepot,* volume VII #4, issue 28, Fall, 1976, pp. 69, 71–72, 74, 76.

————. "An Introduction To Tapestry." *Shuttle, Spindle and Dyepot,* volume VIII #1, issue 29, Winter, 1976, pp. 73, 74–76, 79, 81.

Regensteiner, Else. *Weaver's Study Course, Ideas and Techniques.* New York: Van Nostrand Reinhold, 1975.

Sayler, Mary. *Shuttle, Spindle and Dyepot,* volume III #2, Spring, 1972, p. 31.

Shuttle, Spindle and Dyepot. 4 issues per year. Handweavers Guild of America, Inc., West Hartford, Conn.

Tidball, Harriet. *The Weaver's Book, Fundamentals of Handweaving.* New York: The Macmillan Company, 1962.

Tod, Osma Gallinger, and Del Deo, Josephine Couch. *Rug Weaving For Everyone.* New York: Bramhall House, 1957.

West, Virginia. *Finishing Touches for the Handweaver.* Newton Centre, Mass.: Charles T. Branford Company, 1967.

Worst, Edward F. *Weaving With Foot Powered Looms.* New York: Dover Publications Inc., 1974.

Znamierowski, Nell. *Step-By-Step Weaving.* New York: Golden Press, Inc., 1967.

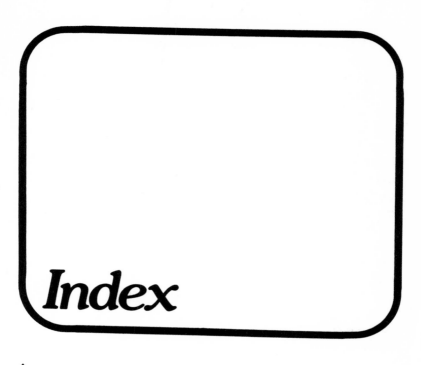

Index

I

inkle band weaves, 88–90
inlay, 130
installation, 163–66
invisible seams, 157–58

J

jack loom, 19
josephine knot, 161, 163
justifying, 84–85
jute, 54

L

lace weaves, 120, 130
lea, 53
lease sticks, 108–9
leno, 130
lighting, 9–10
linen, 53
loom buying, 12
loom frame, 13
loom knots, 23–27
loom maintenance, 36
looms, 12–40
loom tying, 23–35

M

mechanical advantage, 24
metallic yarn, 54
metal wires, 54
mini lease sticks, 107–8
monkey's fist, 161–62
monk's belt, 81–82
M's and O's, 82–83

N

needlework, 133
neolithic knot, 151–52
new warp ends, 117

O

overhand knot, 23, 146–49
overshot, 83–84

P

pattern treadles, 119
pattern weaves, 121
pickup harness, 37
pile techniques, 128–29
place mats, 97, 148
plaiting, 155–56
planning yardage, 95–96
plied cord adjustable knot, 27
plying, 155
pockets, 142–44
pulled loops, 128–29
pumice, 36

R

raddle, 110
raffia, 54
record sheets, 91–92
reeds, 112
reed hook, 112–14
reed marks, 79
repair heddles, 116–17
reversing twills, 80
rolled hem, 156
rosepath, 85
rugs, 128

run, 50
running stitch, 133
rya knots, 67, 128–29

S
scarves, 98
seams, 157–60
seersucker, 55
self facing, 138–39
selvedge flaw, 122
selvedges, 59, 96, 122–24
shawls, 98
shoe strings, 110
short drafts, 83
shrinkage, 104
shuttle race, 16
shuttles, 44, 120–21
silk, 54
single layer double beam,
    102–3
sisal, 54
skeins, 59–60
slash pocket, 142–44
sleying the reed, 112–14
snitch, 25
soumak, 128–29
spool rack, 41, 42–43
spools, 63
square knot, 24, 115
storage, 10–12
string heddle, 16–17,
    116–17
summer and winter, 82
supplementary beam, 37
supplementary warp, 101
Swedish lace, 80
synthetics, 54

T
tabby, 116, 119
takeup, 93–94, 104
tapestry finish, 51
tapestry weave, 89
tapestry weft, 93–94
tassels, 155–56
tensioning the warp, 110
thimble hook, 112
threading corrections,
    116–17
threading drafts, 71–72
threading heddles, 111–12
three-color weft pattern,
    131–32
three-strand flat braid,
    155–56
thrums, 11
tie-up, 16, 71–74
tool box, 48
treadle dancing, 118–19
treadling, 71–74, 118–19,
    126
twice-woven weavings,
    67–70
twill, 78–80, 119, 123, 124,
    127, 128
twining, 128
two-color weft pattern,
    131–32
tying-on, 114–15

W
wall hangings, 128
warp, 105–8
warp breakage, 50
warp dressing, 53